T0208314

Living Happily Ever After

The reward of the Monomythic Journey

WILLIAM OLDFIELD

authorHOUSE

AuthorHouse™
1663 Liberty Drive
Bloomington, IN 47403
www.authorhouse.com
Phone: 833-262-8899

© *2023 William Oldfield. All rights reserved.*

No part of this book may be reproduced, stored in a retrieval system, or transmitted by any means without the written permission of the author.

Published by AuthorHouse   04/27/2023

ISBN: 979-8-8230-0718-4 (sc)
ISBN: 979-8-8230-0720-7 (hc)
ISBN: 979-8-8230-0719-1 (e)

Library of Congress Control Number: 2023907954

Print information available on the last page.

Any people depicted in stock imagery provided by Getty Images are models, and such images are being used for illustrative purposes only. Certain stock imagery © Getty Images.

This book is printed on acid-free paper.

Because of the dynamic nature of the Internet, any web addresses or links contained in this book may have changed since publication and may no longer be valid. The views expressed in this work are solely those of the author and do not necessarily reflect the views of the publisher, and the publisher hereby disclaims any responsibility for them.

Contents

The Crucible of Reality

Preface

We live in an era of massive change on a global scale. In the last one hundred years, there have been more significant changes than in the preceding two thousand years. My father remembers running down the lane of the family farm just to watch a car go by. Now we can see thousands of cars on the freeway going nowhere during rush hour. Our cities are now powered by electricity. Soon we will be able to book a personal holiday into space to witness our cities light up at night. Above all, the invention of the computer chip has been revolutionary. Refrigerators can tell us when our milk supply is running low. Cars can drive themselves while we sleep. Cell phones connect people from all corners of the world, and they have become computers in our pockets.

In the last hundred years, the capitalist economy has created enormous wealth. The changes are endless and amazing, but change is disruptive and not totally good or equally beneficial to all. Unrestricted capitalism has allowed CEOs to move their manufacturing to countries with low wages to return with phenomenally inexpensive goods and phenomenally high returns for their investors. Meanwhile, once thriving cities are now inhabited by vacant, deteriorating factories and the lives of thousands of families have been disrupted. Many factories remain and are still booming. Instead of thousands of workers, there are only a few staff greasing the wheels and tending the robots.

Automation is marvelous. Robots can work 24 hours a day, 7 days a week, and don't take breaks, get sick, or want holidays in the summer. Meanwhile, the lives of thousands who lost their jobs are disrupted. And on top of that, the inequitable distribution of wealth continues to rise. Currently, according to the National Bureau of Economic Research, the richest 5% of Americans own two-thirds of the wealth. The most expensive cars fill the roads of our cities while a huge number of people work two jobs just to feed their families. Most governments, so far, have failed to make the cultural or economic changes necessary to rectify these inequities.

There is one area of significant change that is affecting most of us but without any major downside. This is the area of increasing knowledge about the human animal. Science and scholarly research are laying bare more of the realities of how humans function.

We have decoded the human genome, "a complete set of nucleic acid sequences, encoded as DNA within 23 chromosome pairs in the cell nuclei and in a small DNA molecule found within individual mitochondria". I don't even know what that all means, but it is a complete layout of nature's plan for the creation of a human being. This knowledge promises great strides for the future of medicine. More relevant to the topic of this book is our ever-growing insight into child development, the processes by which a child grows from infancy through adolescence to adulthood.

We are all born into an established culture. As children, we learn enormously complicated concepts in record time. Like sponges, we absorb ideas from our environment to adapt and survive. But this is not reasoned learning. These are ideas and concepts imprinted emotionally in our minds that become the unconscious knowledge that guides us in life. These emotionally ingrained ideas are the perceptual patterns that give meaning to the raw data of our senses. What we see is what we know. Any sensory data that doesn't fit is ignored as noise. We don't even see it. The meaning derived from these perceptual patterns creates the normal, natural, cultural world that we adapted to and inhabit. It is here that we feel most comfortable.

As long as the world confirms our unconscious knowledge, we feel comfortable and at home. If the world changes or our unconscious understanding is challenged, we feel uncomfortable and threatened. Our discomfort prompts our emotions to tell the computer in our head to find out what's going on. The brain races off and analyses the situation in light of all our knowledge and experience. When the brain returns with an answer, the emotions evaluate it. If the answer does not feel right, the brain runs off to try again. But, if it does feel right, an understanding is gained, and the discomfort is dispelled. Truth need not be an attribute of this understanding. Elimination of our discomfort is the objective.

The degree of discomfort depends upon the impact the changes impose on our lives. If minor discomfort arises, we merely seek an understanding so that we can stop thinking about the problem. By contrast, if angst and worry are tearing us apart, the question to the brain is like a scream for help. In response, the brain moves quickly to find an answer to the angst and anguish.

Unfortunately, any answer will do in a storm: "It's those Jews hoarding all the money. It's those blacks and queers destroying our culture. It's those immigrants stealing our jobs." For some men, "it's women that are the cause of all our problems." Finally, we understand, and the angst and torment become anger instead. Righteous anger feels so much better than helpless angst. In this way, xenophobia, homophobia, misogyny, and racism provide convenient scapegoats for our problem, so angry hatred can mitigate our pain.

As a result, in times of disruptive change, we see a significant increase in acts of violence and hatred against innocent people. If we reject all scapegoats, our brain continues looking for the source of the problem and, if no answers feel right, we find no rescue. Desperate to end the dilemma, the brain suggests a final answer: "End it all". Sadly, in times of disruptive change, there is a significant increase in the number of suicides. Such toxic solutions are failures of adaptation. In our current world of rapid and disruptive change, the chaos we experience around us is a product of this failure.

An alternative appears if we reject both scapegoats and suicide as ways to dissipate our angst. It occurs to us that we could try just learning to live with the problem. But shallow tolerance is so stressful that it too has major downsides. Not only does prolonged angst destroy our physical health, but it also makes the achievement of happiness impossible. Since happiness is the primary goal of life, there is only one solution: find an answer within our mind that mitigates the discomfort. We must make an exploratory journey into our mind, a realm of all possibilities, for the answer.

Just such a brave venture into one's inner self is the topic of this book. In mythology, this inner trip is called the "Monomythic Journey". In some areas of study, it's called the "Adaptative Response" and in others the "Creative Act". At its core, the adventure involves the rewiring of our existing mental patterns to incorporate new perspectives. This intense rebuilding process makes the inner journey a personal quest for peace of mind. It is necessarily a highly emotional experience.

Many years ago, I experienced such a transformation through a revelatory variety of the adaptive response. It began with a dramatic emotional event instigated by a crisis in my life. While the crisis, rejection in love, may appear trivial in hindsight, at the time it was not. I was young and in love and believed everything was perfect. Then my world fell apart. She left me. Life became empty and meaningless. There was no hope because she was not coming back. Then, out of a long and painful struggle to extract myself from my depression, I experienced a magical moment. Suddenly I broke out of my dark perceptual cage and my whole life flashed before my eyes. I imaginatively relived, in the reality of human emotional response, pivotal events in my life that had shaped me into the person I'd become, and I saw how my actions precipitated my girlfriend's departure. Suddenly I understood what had happened and liberated from despair, found a whole new world open before me. Everything became wonderful.

This type of experience is often called mystical or religious, but when all the hyperbole is set aside, it is a natural human response to a challenge of adaptation. It occurs when our existing knowledge fails to provide the answer we need. Our agonizing frustration mounts, bursting us out of our locked perspective and casting new light upon the problem. With this new perspective, we are able to understand and devise a solution. The rapid transition from despair to elation imbues the entire experience with a sense of wonder. The answer appears beautiful in its simplicity. We acquire a new perspective that leads to a new understanding that, in my case, helped me adapt to my new reality. An inspirational moment is usually just that, a moment, but in my case, the emotional high lasted for months.

When I tried to tell my friends what was happening to me, it was impossible. At first, the communications gap didn't bother me most of the time because I was having so much fun. But it got to be frustrating since no one could understand what I was going through, and I was not able to explain it properly since I didn't understand it myself. Here was a beautiful and exhilarating experience. I longed to share it, but I didn't know how, and I didn't know anyone who had ever experienced anything similar. I was sure that an experience as wonderful as this could not be unique to me. Coincidentally, as soon as I became convinced that it could not possibly be unique to me, I discovered that it wasn't. I discovered the world of mythology.

Mythologist Joseph Campbell in his book The Hero with a Thousand Faces collected mythic tales from around the world to illustrate that beneath the diversity, each hero's adventure follows a common pattern. He named this standard path the Monomyth. Its pattern is basic to all adventure myths, and to most human experiences of change.

> A hero ventures forth from the world of common day into a region of supernatural wonder: fabulous forces are there encountered, and a decisive victory is won: the hero comes back from this mysterious adventure with the power to bestow boons on his fellow man. (Campbell, Hero with a Thousand Faces, 30)

Latent, if not explicit, in Campbell's thesis is that this mythic region of supernatural wonder is equivalent, in psychological terms, to the realm of the human mind. These early storytellers did not have a psychological vocabulary to discuss their experiences, so they used fantasy to convey common psychological truths.

The realm of the mind is a realm of dreams and nightmares. It is also the realm of the imagination where the laws of nature do not apply. Like Campbell's mythic realm, the realm of the human mind is a "region of supernatural wonder where fabulous forces can be encountered".

During my crisis, I was amazed to see again and again mythic stories that paralleled the exact psychological events I was experiencing. The storylines followed emotional patterns, which, when I empathized with the mythic characters, would call to my mind parallel events from my own experience with similar emotional coloring. As if a neon sign were flashing in my mind, I understood what the author of the myth was describing. The result was a radically new understanding, a new way of looking at the contents of my own experience, as well as an entirely new appreciation for the value of mythology. I realized that many myths and folktales are attempts, using fantasy and fiction as metaphors, to delineate the wild psychological experience of inspiration. I learned that a very real yet mythic happening known as a Meeting with the Goddess represents that moment of inspiration. Its significance reshapes everything. It is transformative.

This innate Adaptive Response is the source of much that we value most in human culture. The Monomythic hero ventures forth from the world of common day into a region of supernatural wonder where fabulous forces are encountered, and a decisive victory is won. Similarly, the human being's innate creative genius dives into the realm of their mind, an inner region where fabulous forces are encountered, and new understanding is devised. In other words, both a mythic protagonist and an everyday person faced with a crisis or unexpected challenge needs to deal with "fabulous forces" and respond with newborn understanding.

> And without the more spectacular exploratory dives of the creative individual, there would be no science and no art.' Koestler, The Creative Act, 181

The powerful creative act is the source of Campbell's Monomyth and the source of humankind's greatest achievements. Our mythic heritage is littered with insights into this process.

Joseph Campbell's Monomyth provides the blueprint for this book. Certain common psychological barriers must be overcome before our creativity can flourish. We'll explore the cage of Mythlock that blinds us to new possibilities. We'll see how Scapegoatism hijacks the emotional harbingers of the creative process and vents them through anger upon any handy external entity. We'll confront the Threshold Guardians of fear that bar the threshold crossing. And we will see how if confidence is lacking, a Magic Amulet eases our passage.

Our first trial across the Garden's threshold is to face the Looking Glass. In front of the Looking Glass, we confront the unleashed emotions of guilt, regret, and anger. Our emotions must be groomed for safe navigation because, within the Garden of the Goddess, negative emotions can breed monsters of the mind. A negative response to new ideas can transform the Goddess into a Hag. A negative attitude towards our own sensuality can transform the Goddess of promise into a Seductrice tempting us into sin and depravity. The climax of the Adventure is an encounter with the Goddess in all her splendor. Everything becomes clear and an answer is manifest in all its beauty and simplicity. But the Goddess always promises more. Beyond the Goddess lies the Stairway to the Stars. This is "Nirvana", a god-like perspective where "All is One". In religious mythology, this is called seeing the face of god.

But the greatest challenge of all is yet to come. The wonderful, exciting, and innovative ideas hatched within the realm of the mind are as nothing until they have passed through the Crucible of Reality. The real test of our gains from our Monomythic Adventure comes with the Return, when we take the Boon, those powerful insights we discovered within the Garden, and put them to actual use in our real day-to-day life. The Challenges of the Return are formidable. Enthusiasm is usually the first casualty. What takes a mere moment to transpire in the fluid realm of the mind can take forever to make happen in the real world.

The world has its successful Monomythic adventurers, its geniuses. These Masters of Two Worlds trip lightly back and forth across the threshold "not contaminating the principles of the one with those of the other, yet permitting the mind to know the one by virtue of the other" (Campbell 229). These geniuses, be they renowned high achievers or quiet unsung heroes known only to their family and friends, have one great feature in common: they revel in the pleasures of new perspectives. For them the creative act is habitual. They understand the tentative nature of knowledge and avoid the trap of the Mythlock. And the Masters of Two Worlds never forget the purpose of the Adventure: to adapt successfully to life's changes and challenges and to help others to do the same. In the words of the fairy tale, they are able, come what may, "to live happily ever after." A key revelation of mythic tales is that all that we think we know and believe is a rationalized creation or fantasy of our conscious mind, a vision deemed adequate by the feelings of our heart. It is a humbling realization that our conscious mind is merely a tool in the service of our emotions. Yet it is also empowering to know that if the rationalized fantasy that we believe is not yet achieving its objective – the creation of a successful, happy life -- all we need do is book ourselves in for another Monomythic Adventure.

Frustration to Inspiration

The Creative Act

When all the hyperbole is set aside, at its core the creative act is merely a natural response to a challenge of adaptation when existing knowledge and experience prove inadequate for the task at hand.

"Eureka," an English word derived from the Greek word meaning, "I found it," is used to express the exuberance of discovery. In the ancient city of Syracuse, the tyrant Hiero received a crown purported to have been made of pure gold, but he suspected the jeweler of adulterating it with silver. He called upon Archimedes, his resident genius, to resolve the issue without destroying the crown. Archimedes knew that the volumes of equal weights of gold and silver were different, but how could he test them and keep the crown intact? He pondered the question for some time in vain. One day, while lowering himself into his bath, Archimedes observed the water rise as his body was immersed. In this repeatable event, he saw a pattern that would provide a solution to his problem with the crown.

The story is that Archimedes leaped from his tub and raced naked through the streets of Syracuse shouting, "Eureka! Eureka!" [I found it! I found it!]. Archimedes realized that he could place the irregular shaped crown in water, measure the water displaced, and compare it to the displacement of water of an equal weight of pure gold. If the amount of water displaced was the same in both cases, then the crown was pure gold. If the amount was not equal, then the jeweler's duplicity would be revealed. In short, Archimedes, troubled by a problem, suddenly saw it in a new light and the solution popped into his mind. This process is the creative act, the "eureka phenomenon" of psychology.

The creative act is not limited to the super-intelligent like Archimedes. It is a natural function of the human brain. For example, as a young student, I remember working on a math problem where the answer eluded me completely. I tried several approaches, but nothing worked. Frustrated and angry, I stormed out of my bedroom. After declaring to my parents that math was stupid and that I would never use it in real life, I returned to my room to face the problem once more. When I looked at it this time, there was the answer, right in front of my eyes. I was elated. The solution was so simple that I felt embarrassed that I hadn't seen it earlier. After an angry distraction resulted in a calmer state of mind, I gained a new perspective on the problem, and the solution was clear. This emotional mental behavior is a familiar cognitive pattern and an innate capability of every human being.

Einstein, an acknowledged genius of the 20th century, is purported to have offered advice on the creation of intelligent children. The folklorist Jack Zipes turns this advice into a short fable in the introduction to his 1979 book, *Breaking the Magic Spell: Radical Theories of Folk and Fairy Tales.*

> Once upon a time, the famous physicist Albert Einstein was confronted by an overly concerned woman who sought advice on how to raise her small son to become a successful scientist. In particular, she wanted to know what kinds of books she should read to her son.

"Fairy Tales," Einstein responded without hesitation.

"Fine, but what else should I read to him after that?" the mother asked.

"More fairy tales," Einstein stated.

"And after that?"

"Even more fairy tales," replied the great scientist, and he waved his pipe like a wizard pronouncing a happy end to a long adventure.

There is a common pattern underlying all fairy tales. The hero encounters a need that must be fulfilled and takes off on his or her adventure to find it. All kinds of challenges are encountered and overcome until the hero finds what he or she needs and then returns home to live happily ever after. The reading of fairy tales to a child introduces this pattern, the Creative Act, to the young mind. The more exposure provided through fairy tales read, the more powerfully the pattern of problem-solving is burnt into a child's mind. The child grasps fully that if you want to solve a dilemma, this is a pattern worth following.

Science today is exploring early childhood development and discovering its critical importance. Concepts of how things work get imprinted emotionally in the mind of a child from an extremely young age. Our emotionally ingrained ideas form the perceptual patterns that give meaning to the raw data of our senses. They provide a meaningful understanding of the world we inhabit. Knowledge acquired through imagined experience, like reading fairy tales, also becomes part of our unconscious reservoir of inner wisdom that guides us in life and, to some extent, represents who we become as we mature. In this way, a child enriched by fairy tales learns that the creative act leads to problem-solving and gains a deeply rooted life skill and vital intelligence.

In the popular *Jack and the Beanstalk* fairy tale adapted from a 1700s folktale, Jack's life is not going anywhere, so he takes a big risk, he trades the family cow for a handful of magic beans. The beans grow into a towering beanstalk reaching up into the clouds. But there's a new problem: since the cow is gone, Jack needs money to feed his family. He climbs the stalk and at the top, he finds himself in the castle of a mean ogre. Avoiding detection, he searches the place and finds some gold coins. Grabbing the coins Jack flees the castle, returns home, and uses the money to feed his family. Of course, the gold runs out and Jack has a new need, a source of steady income for his family, so up he goes again, and this time he finds the goose that lays the golden eggs. Again, he flees the castle and returns home with his family's needs are now satisfied. But Jack is still not satisfied. He feels there is more to life than sleeping and eating so Jack once again climbs the beanstalk and enters the ogre's castle. This time Jack finds the ogre falling asleep to the sweet music of a magic harp. Jack has found what he needs to enrich his life. He grabs the harp, the harp screams, and the ogre awakes, Jacks flees down the beanstalk, grabs an axe, and cuts down the beanstalk. The ogre falls to his demise. It's a wonderful classic tale, satisfying to children and adults alike. I will always remember gazing at the final picture in the Jack and the Beanstalk book I enjoyed in my youth: there stood Jack, his wife, and their child together with huge smiles, the perfect picture of a family living happily ever after.

In real life, of course, the need for creative action occurs many more times than three as we struggle to achieve a happily ever after life. This basic creative pattern happens often in the behavior of young children. They naturally inhabit a world where most things are beyond the scope of their existing knowledge and experience. You can see the occasional "eureka" smiles on their faces whenever they figure something out. Within the first three to five years of life, a child creates a large repertoire of knowledge and experience, establishing a resource that helps him or her understand and interact with their environment. Children are learning sponges. Their minds are open, their curiosity boundless, and they are constantly exploring the world around them. Science is discovering the enormous importance of early childhood in the development of a properly functioning adult human being.

We consult our library of unconscious knowledge and experience constantly. The process goes something like this. In any given situation our feelings are the sensors we use to take stock. The feelings aroused in a given situation call to mind past events from our repertoire of knowledge and experience that have similar emotional coloring. It is as if our knowledge is indexed by our feelings. Enter a room filled with people we know and like, and there is a feeling of familiarity and comfort. From previous experience, we know how to behave in this environment. Enter the same room with several strangers present, and we feel slightly different, perhaps curious or intrigued. If upon entering the room we encounter someone we detest, the feelings aroused are distinctive and our response is adjusted as appropriate. In any given situation, our feelings are the sensors we use to take stock. These aroused feelings call to mind past events from our repertoire of knowledge and experience that have similar emotional coloring. This recalled knowledge provides an understanding of the situation, or at least one close enough to allow us to react appropriately. This is how we use our existing knowledge and experience to function every day. It normally happens so fast that we are hardly aware of it.

Once any behavioral pattern is learned and proves successful, we tend to rely on it and use it again and again in similar situations. When these learned responses work out well, again and again, they become habitual. Our minds are, in fact, habit-making machines. Once we have figured something out and this understanding is useful in helping us function, we call upon it again and again. In this way we can interact with our worlds, most of the time, without having to consciously figure out every step along the way. Through this strategy, our conscious minds are freed up for more important matters. This is the norm. Each of us has a large repertoire of knowledge and experience created over time that we tap into to guide our actions.

But what happens when our existing knowledge proves inadequate in a new situation? What happens when we don't understand and don't know what to do? When our existing knowledge and experience fail us, the situation demands a fresh response. It requires a creative act. Discomfort and anxiety flare when we encounter situations that we do not understand. The desire to escape these unpleasant feelings provides the incentive for us to break free from our automatic responses. Discomfort and anxiety are the harbingers of the creative act. They stimulate the creative response. Suddenly through some miracle of the mind, the habitual blinders are removed, and we see the problem in a new light. This new perspective reveals new options and new possibilities, allowing our conscious minds to devise a new, and hopefully, appropriate response. In the process, our discomfort is dispelled. This is the simple emotional pattern of the creative act. Its gift to us is a pleasurable feeling of accomplishment.

When the challenge we face has great importance to us and the discomfort is more intense, the intensity of the relief is also much greater. In that case, we give the experience a new name: it becomes an inspirational moment. Most of us have, at some point in our lives, experienced a flash of insight, an inspirational moment. Besides the simple problem-solving and the more intense inspirational moments, there is yet another level of intensity and again we give it a new name. When it is not a simple problem or challenge that we face but a crisis in our lives, the emotional intensity tends to transform the event into something that may look different, but the same underlying emotional pattern remains. In these situations, we can feel hopelessly trapped in a crisis without resolution. Unlike the simple problem-solving situation where a moment's distraction may precede a breakthrough, in these highly emotional instances the critical moment is often reached when the struggle to understand ceases and we consciously surrender. Then, suddenly through some miracle of the mind, we are freed from our habitual perspective, and we see our situation in a new light. Whatever the specifics of that critical moment, the transition can be dramatic. Suddenly the world we perceive is transformed and we can be immersed in wonder and awe. This manifestation of the creative act we call a revelatory experience.

The intense revelatory varieties of the creative act are the ones that interest us most because these are life-transforming events. Attempts to describe these wild revelatory experiences vary in detail but often mention a mind/body separation as if floating above and looking down upon our own bodies. This extreme reaction has also been described as seeing our life flashing before our eyes. Like viewing a movie, we get to watch and re-experience emotionally seminal events in our lives, the ones that shaped us into the persons we've become. We come to know ourselves.

One purpose of this self-evaluation process is to help us understand the limits of our existing understanding. We can re-examine our existing habitual understandings and break out of our perceptual box and see things in a new light. Unlike a mild inspirational moment, these wild revelatory experiences are often imbued with mystical or even religious overtones. But when all the hyperbole is set aside, at its core this experience is merely a natural response to a challenge of adaptation, the simple yet potentially powerful creative act.

I experienced one of the wilder revelatory varieties of the creative experience many years ago. If my experience was unique in any way, it was not because of its emotional intensity but because it did not last just a few minutes like most inspirational events. The emotional intensity fades once a solution or understanding arises for the problem at hand. While I did gain an insight into the challenge I faced, the emotional intensity of the experience rendered the solution to my problem insignificant in light of the experience itself. The revelatory experience rather than a solution became my focus. As a result, my experience lasted for over three months. I was higher than a kite because something truly remarkable happens at the moment of revelation. The mind becomes fluid. If the inspirational moment fails to provide a prompt answer, the mind can remain fluid. From this continuing fluidity of mind, fresh ideas flow. This fluidity of mind is the heart of the revelatory experience. For three months, if I had a question, in a flash I had an answer. At times the ideas were profound and awe-inspiring, yet in other cases, they were just plain stupid. It was a wonderfully exciting time.

Ideas blossomed freely, and I followed wherever they lead. Sailing smoothly, a question, a moment's doubt, and suddenly the wind changed and – like a wind surfer turning on a dime – I was off in a new direction following a new wind. I experienced weeks of varying degrees of unrestrained creativity. I saw ten solutions to a single problem in the flash of an eye. There was nothing, I believed, that could escape understanding if I just focused my attention on it. No one around me could understand what I was going through at the time, and I couldn't explain it properly. I think my friends thought that I had lost my mind, but they were polite about it. When it was happening, I didn't understand it myself. Eventually, at an auspicious point, I turned my focus inward upon the experience itself. I studied the events that preceded my moment of revelation to figure out what had happened and how it came to trigger such a glorious mental event. Looking back with attention, I reviewed the story of my recent past.

Back at its start, I was a student living a great life, and then I met her and my great life became a really great life. I was introduced to love and all the wondrous feelings it unleashes. I didn't know what was going on, but it was wonderful. I was happy, but then trouble entered paradise. At a party, she would start an argument while all I wanted to do was have a good time. She was obsessed with our making a life-long commitment, but we were both far too young for long-term plans. For me, these days were a time for living, not worrying about the future. I felt that her obsession was at the root of all our trouble. When she left me, I remember blaming her, trying to convince myself that I was better off without her. This attitude brought me some relief, but it was short-lived. I loved her, so trying to dump all the blame for our problems on her was useless. Whenever thoughts of her entered my mind, memories of all our good times flooded back. Blaming her resolved nothing, and I slipped deeper into depression.

I saw that some of our worst fights occurred when I was less than sober. We would be having a good time; she would make some comment and my flippant, uninhibited tongue would blurt out things that hurt her. She would respond in kind and the fight was on. This was an answer; this was the source of our problem. I became convinced that I was an alcoholic. I skipped several parties and stayed sober, but, if anything, sober self-imposed isolation only made me more depressed.

Trying to figure out the real source of our problem, I looked at the main frustrations in my life. I was always worried about money. Student loans, two jobs, and still, I could hardly manage. I was always having to beg and borrow to survive. I never had enough money to take her places or to buy her nice things. My frustration would often pop up in the middle of one of our arguments. My lack of money was a constant irritant. Money, I decided, was the source of our problem. The love of money, after all, is said to be the root of all evil. I saw that the whole damn capitalist system, which valued people more for what they had than who they were, was a screwed-up system. Any relief I felt from this explanation was fleeting because, when I thought about it honestly, I was always broke. I was broke when I met her; I was broke when we were having our great times together; and I was still broke. Blaming our problems on my lack of money didn't resolve anything, and I remained depressed.

As I re-examined this period of my life, when I was trying to figure out what had gone wrong in our relationship, I noticed a subtle change taking place in the process. Anger would rescue me momentarily from depression whenever I identified a source of blame for our troubles. Then some doubt that I had the right answer would enter the picture, and I would reject that solution and slip once more into depression. A week passed between the time I first blamed her for our problem and my switching the blame to my abusing alcohol. But the time between identifying a source of blame for the problem and the rejection of the solution began to diminish. The insights were coming faster.

I thought about all my inculcated values around sex, love, marriage, and commitment that my parents had instilled in me. Love was a new experience. New hormones were racing through my veins and, although it was wonderful, it was unsettling. I didn't know how to act. I discovered a conflict between what I had been taught and the reality of my relationship with her. An idea that my parents had instilled in me was that "When you love someone and you have sex with that someone, you have to commit to that person for life. If you don't, you are just using them for your own selfish pleasure." But we were too young for any permanent commitment, and abstinence was out of the question. If I had abstained, she would have left me sooner. My problem was caused by a conflict between the beliefs I held and the reality of my relationship with my girlfriend.

Here was a new target for my blaming game: my parents were at fault for imposing on me their stupid morality. My parents had screwed up my upbringing and created this problem. How often have we heard that refrain? Any relief felt at this false solution was gone in a flash because my mind was picking up speed, and I loved my parents. It wasn't fair to blame this on them. Besides, I realized that my parents were trapped in the same stupid morality. They had been sold the same bill of goods. Religion was the source of these ideas. Religion propagated a morality that was totally out of sync with the reality of human nature. The priests and ministers of the world were the sources of the problem. But before I could vent any anger on them, I realized that they too were individuals trapped in the same belief system. Where did these ideas come from? Finally, I had the answer: god was the source, a source upon which I could safely vent all my anger and frustration.

I remember sneaking out of a party without my coat and wandering through the field behind the apartment knee-deep in snow whipped by howling winds. I screamed at god for his stupidity in creating such a senseless and confusing world. I vented my anger and frustration at the black clouds sweeping across the sky until I was hoarse. When I stopped, tears burnt my eyes, and I realized that still nothing was resolved. I remember dropping to my knees in the snow and feeling myself sink deeper and deeper into despair. With all my thrashing about in search of an answer, I found nothing that helped me escape my dilemma. I was caught in a pit of despair, and there was no way out. Suicide did arise as a solution, but I rejected it out of hand as a stupid idea.

Then it happened. I surrendered to the helplessness of the situation and in an unguarded moment of introspection, I saw myself. Clearly for the very first time. I saw myself fall in love and open up like the petals of a flower, then immediately put on a mask of flippant uncaring to hide my vulnerability. Seeing the mask, she thought I didn't care. She thought I didn't care, and I was the one who gave her that impression. I realized I was the author of the misconceptions and misunderstandings that caused our problem. I was the author of my own misfortunes. With revelation comes liberation. The depression that had held me in its grasp for weeks suddenly dissipated. Now I understood.

Where depression and confusion had reigned, all was suddenly clear and so simple that it was beautiful. As I learned later, in mythic terminology, I had received a "gift from the Goddess", a new life perspective that revealed an answer to the question I sought. But the Goddess always promises more. My mind was fluid and suddenly, not just those incidents relevant to the immediate crisis, but my whole life flashed before my eyes. I relived, in the reality of human emotional response, those events in my life that had molded me into the person I'd become, and it was not all pretty. I saw myself free from all self-deceiving illusions. I winced in pain as I relived instances where I had, through stupidity, inflicted hurt upon others. I felt their pain as my own. Eventually, I found forgiveness and was launched on the true Adventure of a lifetime.

The ecstasy of the moment of revelation is exquisite. All that is dull and boring is transformed and suffused with novelty. A whole new world opens up in front of our eyes. We become like children again, seeing everything for the first time. The blinders of habitual perspectives are removed; the mind becomes fluid; we see everything in a new light and new options and new possibilities are revealed. This emotional pattern is so simple yet so powerful. We encounter a situation beyond the scope of our existing knowledge and experience and we don't know what to do. This uncertainty causes discomfort. Escape from this discomfort becomes the incentive to break out of our habitual perceptual box. The moment of inspiration is the moment of break out. Our minds are liberated from the trap of habit, and we discover a new way of looking at things. This new perspective reveals new options and new possibilities so our conscious minds can devise new understanding that leads to the development of a new adaptive strategy.

The "ah hah!" or "eureka" phenomenon is the creative act in action. Increase the emotional intensity of the creative act and we give it new names. We call it inspiration or revelation. The wildest, life-transforming manifestations of the creative act we call mystical or religious. But the same emotional pattern lies at the core of all these experiences regardless of what we call them.

It is important to recognize that the creative act is an innate talent. Each of us possesses within us this creative tool, which is capable of rescuing us from the most devastatingly hopeless psychological crises and even the most physically challenging situations. Its purpose is clear. Its purpose is survival. Its purpose is successful adaptation. This is how we adapt, succeed and create a wonderful life for ourselves and those around us. But we need to understand the vagaries of the creative act to use it successfully. Thankfully, the creative act is a well-trodden and well-documented path so we can learn its intricacies without having to blunder through the experience the way I did. For centuries, individuals who have experienced these exciting emotional events have documented them for us to read. These lessons, in countless variations, are documented in our mythological heritage.

Our Mythic Heritage

Myths and folktales are descriptions of psychological experiences and our mythic heritage, a manual of the mind.

A revelatory experience is one of the most exciting psychological events. It is emotionally charged and can be life-transforming. Because it is a personal experience the specifics of each situation vary wildly. The explanation devised by the conscious mind to describe or attempt to explain this inner experience varies even more widely because it draws upon an individual's unique knowledge and experience to create the context for the explanation. Because there is no concrete external reality to psychological events, an individual must also use their imagination to draw it together. As a result, the variety of descriptions of inspirational or revelatory experiences is unlimited.

Imagine for a moment the death of one we love who is the center of our existence. We are devastated. The future is empty. Where a loving smile once filled our lives there is now nothing but a big black hole of despair. We struggle to come to grips with this new reality but to no avail. There is no hope. Death is final. We surrender to despair until suddenly by some miracle of the mind we experience a revelation. While the emotional pattern underlying a revelatory experience may be common, the specifics of the event are always varied, as are the images and ideas used to describe the event. In the example of the death of a loved one, one person with a secular orientation could interpret the experience as the gaining of a new perspective leading to a better accommodation with the realities of life and death. Another individual steeped in religious mythology could just as easily interpret the same experience as a message from god showing the defeat of death and the reality of heaven and life everlasting. The more dramatic instances of an adaptive response are highly emotional and when the conscious mind goes to work trying to make sense of these experiences, the images, ideas, and explanations vary widely.

As I continued my research it became clear to me that mythology, at least a major portion of mythology, was the language of psychology before psychology was invented. The necessity of using fantasy and fiction for the discussion of psychological experiences is obvious. How do you describe something that is transpiring within your mind? Talking about synapses firing or wonder and awe without context makes for poor communication. It is only mythically, through the use of stories and images that it becomes possible to discuss or describe inner emotional/mental events. Emotion is the core of the inspirational event, and you can't talk about emotions effectively without context. So, metaphor, stories, and images become the currency for the sharing of internal emotional experiences. Even modern psychology uses mythology to describe psychosis. We have the Oedipus complex, love for the mother and jealousy for the father, or the self-absorption of Narcissism. Psychological researchers are constantly using mythological references to describe mental states because they recognize emotional parallels between the patterns of the stories and psychological events. Our mythic heritage from this perspective becomes a vast resource of descriptions of psychological experiences collected over the ages.

I found story after story that described what I was going through. It seems a very large portion of our Mythic Heritage describes the creative experience. It is also amazing how comforting it felt at the time to realize that I was not alone. Hundreds of thousands of people through the ages have had similar experiences and many of them recorded theirs in folktales or mythological stories. But my amazement was not just for the portions of the stories that paralleled my experiences. After all, I discovered that the mind becomes fluid during the revelatory process, and with a fluid mind, anything becomes possible. As a result, through empathy, I was now able to emotionally experience events that were new to me. I was able to virtually live new experiences. Since many of the mythical tales were warnings about traps, psychologically dangerous or foolish reactions arising out of the creative experience, experiencing them virtually was a lot easier than living them in painful reality. At one point I became curious about what it was that I was doing while reading mythic tales that triggered these flashes of insight. Why were these weird stories suddenly blossoming full of meaning within my mind? What was I doing?

I realized as I approached a mythic tale that I was emotionally empathizing with the characters in the story. It seems that an open empathetically emotional state is a characteristic if not synonymous with a fluid mind. I was attempting to feel as the characters felt to feel as I would feel in their situations. The storylines followed an emotional pattern experienced by the character and by empathizing with the character I was virtually living their story, experiencing it in the reality of human emotional response. To feel as another feels is to know as another knows. When you feel as another feels you can understand the emotional source of their actions and reactions. This is the essence of what it means to walk a mile in another's shoes. This is how we can understand others and also how we can penetrate the meaning that the authors of mythology were attempting to communicate. The feelings aroused in the process called to mind past events from my repertoire of knowledge and experience that had similar emotional coloring. Suddenly I was seeing my own experience in the context of the mythic tale. The fantasy content of the story provided the context for the inner emotional pattern. Parallels between my experience and the mythic tale became obvious. The parallels were in the emotional pattern. Once I recognized what I was doing, connecting emotionally, I figured out why mythology, a vast resource of depictions of psychological experiences, was hidden in plain sight.

I was using an emotional approach to mythology that gives rise to interpretations sympathetic to the mythic character. The standard scholarly interpretations of mythic stories arise from a much different strategy. The standard, western, scholarly approach to mythology is that of an objective observer. Scholars in non-emotional, coolly objective ways examine the facts. They examine the acts and reactions of the mythic hero from the outside. The interpretations produced from this approach are radically different from those derived from the empathic or emotional approach. Nowhere is the difference in interpretation arising from these diverse approaches more clearly evident than in the familiar Narcissus myth. The Narcissus myth is about a character, Narcissus, who sees himself reflected in a pool of clear water and according to the standard interpretation, falls madly in love with himself. The objective approach sees a self-indulgent, arrogant young man ruining his life through his own obsession. On the other hand, the emotional approach to the Narcissus story reveals a description of a revelatory experience with a warning of one potential conscious response to avoid because it leads to a dead end.

The standard interpretation of the Narcissus myth is that Narcissus fell in love with himself. The dictionary defines "narcissism" as "a morbid condition characterized by excessive admiration of oneself, one's person, abilities, etc. (Universal Dictionary 761). This modern, worldwide interpretation arises from the objective approach to the study of the Narcissus myth. The story is viewed from the perspective of an outside observer. This objective observer sees a character that becomes enamored with his image and ruins his life because of it. It is quite clear from this perspective that Narcissus suffers from a mental aberration.

Lost in the objective approach is any delineation of the emotional pattern that lies at the heart of the inner experience the storyteller is communicating. With an empathetic approach to mythology, you immerse yourself in the story. Empathetically you attempt to feel as the character feels to understand as the character understands. This approach realizes that the essence of what is being communicated through the mythic tale is an inner emotional/mental experience, which can only be understood by feeling as the mythic character feels. This approach produces a much different understanding of the mythic character than the objective approach because you feel the emotional source from which the character's actions and reactions arise.

What I saw through the emotional approach to the Narcissus myth was a description of an emotionally intense creative experience. The story starts with the prophecy of Tiresias that Narcissus will live a long life if only he does not 'come to know himself.' Narcissus is a young man who has the world by the tail. He is rich, intelligent, and handsome and all the girls adore him. Sadly, there was no parallel in my life to this part of the story. The initiating event of the Narcissus experience was also quite different from mine. Many different situations in a person's life can lead to a revelatory event.

> Under the effect of some overwhelming experience, the hero is made to realize the shallowness of his life, the futility, and the frivolity of the daily pursuits of man in the

> trivial routines of existence. This realization may come to him as a sudden shock caused by some catastrophic event, or as the cumulative effect of a slow inner development, or through the trigger action of some banal experience that assumes an unexpected significance. The hero then suffers a crisis that involves the very foundations of his being; he embarks on the Night Journey and is suddenly transferred to the Tragic Plane -- from which he emerges purified, enriched by new insight, and regenerated on a higher level of integration. (Koestler 358)

My youthful revelation was triggered by an "apparently banal experience", of young love, while Narcissus' appears to have been the result of "a slow inner development" or disillusionment with life.

In the story Narcissus has everything going for him yet he is discontent. He has everything we could imagine that a person could want yet for Narcissus something is lacking. His discontent is the harbinger of the Adventure to come. Narcissus realizes the shallowness of his life of leisure, he suffers from the "Is that all there is?" syndrome. Narcissus looks around at all he has and asks himself, "Is that all there is? Is this all that life has to offer? There has to be more!" Narcissus is a young man searching for meaning. "What is the purpose of my life? Why am I here?" In his search, Narcissus wanders off into a strange and peaceful place.

> There was a clear pool, with shining silvery waters, where shepherds had never made their way; no goats that pasture on the mountains, no cattle had ever come there. Its peace was undisturbed by bird or beast or falling branches. (Ovid 85)

This is no natural place. A woodland setting undisturbed by birds or beasts or falling branches is impossible. This is a symbolic realm. What do we do in moments of solitude? We think about things; we speculate; we daydream. We enter the magical realm of the mind where natural laws do not apply. This is the realm of all possibilities. This is a realm of the unfettered imagination.

In this state of reverie, Narcissus suddenly sees himself reflected in a "clear pool with shining silvery waters." He sees himself in a natural Looking Glass and the moment is an imagistic equivalent to the psychological event of mind/body separation. Narcissus steps outside of himself and sees himself. But the prophecy was not simply what would happen if Narcissus saw himself but if he "came to know himself." Coming to know ourselves is the essence of the event when our lives flash before our eyes, which is a frequent first step. Watching the seminal events in our lives and reliving them emotionally, we discover how we were molded by events and ideas into the person we've become. This is "coming to know ourselves".

Reflected in "shining silvery water" Narcissus comes to know himself. This is an imagistic or mythic description of the moment of revelation, the moment we break out and acquire a new perspective. The emotions of this moment are wonderful. Even the word ecstasy can be an inadequate description. The emotions of the moment can be greater than the rush experienced by a drug addict, but alas the moment passes.

The feelings pass, and we come down from our high, but the desire to re-experience that moment does not diminish. Narcissus yearns to re-establish that feeling and his frustration is increased by the knowledge that only some trick of mind and emotion prevents it from happening.

> nor yet highways or mountains, or city walls
> with close-barred gates. ... How I wish I could
> separate myself from my body. (Ovid 86)

Narcissus yearns for a repeat of this mind/body separation experience, but it is not to be. He goes on to beat himself black and blue, much like some individuals do during certain religious festivals, to provoke the mystical experience. Narcissus does not give up. He continues his futile efforts to revisit this emotional state. Herein lies the lesson of the creator of this mythic tale. If you experience the ecstasy of a dramatic revelatory event, enjoy it but get on with your life because the wildly fluid state of mind precipitated by a revelatory event is extremely difficult to reinitiate once lost and it will never again be as dramatic as it was the first time.

The Narcissus myth when approached emotionally is seen as a description of a revelatory experience. But the creator of the mythic tale also provided a lesson I had not yet learned. The fluidity of mind arising from a revelatory event cannot last. A creative frenzy is not a state compatible with sane and sober functioning. At the end of my three months of creative frenzy when I grounded out and came back down to earth, initially I didn't realize what I had lost. Initially, I didn't even know it was over. Once realized, unlike Narcissus, I did not beat myself black and blue to reinitiate the experience, but I did try meditation. I did try to re-establish that state but from the Narcissus myth, I learned the lesson of the author. I used the lessons learned from the myth, gave up any obsession with re-establishing that feeling of ecstasy, and got on with my life.

Again, and again myths and folktales provided me with new insights into my experience. Not only did they provide descriptions of events I was experiencing but related possibilities that I had not experienced. In some cases, the possibilities described, like in the Narcissus myth, were possibilities to be avoided. Myth and folktale are descriptions of psychological events. Now I understood why these apparently childish stories hold such fascination. Our Mythic Heritage turns out to be a vast manual of the mind, a treasure trove of insights into the emotional/mental nature of the human animal. Our Mythic Heritage is a jungle of stories covering multiple topics collected from around the world and throughout the ages. Luckily, I found a guide through the jungle. Joseph Campbell in his book, The Hero with a Thousand Faces, describes the Monomythic Journey. He shows that mythic tales from around the world offer us imagistic access to the meaning-rich emotional/mental pattern of the creative act.

The Monomythic Journey

The Monomythic Journey is an imagistic description of the emotional pattern inherent in the creative act.

Everyone should be familiar with the emotional pattern inherent in the creative experience. Everyone should also be familiar with some of the more dramatic varieties of the creative experience. That way, if it happens to them, they will understand what the hell is going on. I didn't have a clue, and as a result, I found the experience to be more traumatic than it has to be. Only by luck did I escape some major traps. My knowledge of the nature of the creative experience was minimal, limited to the notion that it was something that artists undergo in the act of creating beautiful pictures, inspiring music, or meaning-laden lines of poetry. I would never have guessed that this natural human experience was important to our survival and happiness. When it happened to me, I didn't understand, but very much wished to do so. Determined to find out, I started researching the issue. My curiosity led me to discover an almost limitless resource of examples and descriptions of the inspirational process. In the works of Joseph Campbell, I discovered the secret treasure of mythology. Joseph Campbell was a renowned scholar of comparative mythology and religion and a popular American lecturer in the 1970s and 80s. In studying the seemingly chaotic variety of our worldwide mythic heritage, Campbell noticed an underlying storyline that ties all adventure tales together. In his 1949 book, The Hero with a Thousand Faces, he identified a common pattern that repeats itself in mythological tales from around the world and throughout the ages. He called this timeless pattern the 'Monomyth'.

> The standard path of the mythical adventure of the hero is a magnification of the formula represented in the rites of passage: separation -- initiation – return: which might be named the nuclear unit of the Monomyth.

> A hero ventures forth from the world of common day into a region of supernatural wonder: fabulous forces are there encountered and a decisive victory is won: the hero comes back from this mysterious adventure with the power to bestow boons on his fellow man. Prometheus ascended to the heavens, stole fire from the gods, and descended. Jason sailed through the Clashing Rocks into the sea of marvels, circumvented the dragon that guarded the Golden Fleece and returned with the fleece and the power to wrest his rightful throne from a usurper. (Campbell 30)

The Monomythic Journey or adventure begins when the hero is confronted with a crisis for which there is no solution at hand. All the familiar responses prove inadequate. A new response is required. An answer must be sought beyond the familiar. The hero must "venture forth from the world of common day into a region of supernatural wonder". The emotions of these initiating moments can range from discomfort, anxiety, frustration, and despair, to the deepest, darkest depression.

> The herald or announcer of the adventure, therefore, is often dark, loathly, or terrifying, judged evil by the world; yet if one could follow, the way would be opened through the walls of

day into the dark where the jewels glow. Or the herald is a beast (as in the fairy tale), representative of the repressed instinctual fecundity within ourselves, or again a veiled mysterious figure -- the unknown. (Campbell 53)

Discomfort, anxiety, and despair are the emotional harbingers of the Monomythic adventure. Because these are uncomfortable feelings, they are symbolized by dark and loathly creatures. These strange creatures prod and entice the hero to leave the familiar and venture into the unknown. These creatures, symbolic of feelings of discomfort, provide the impetus that drives the hero forward on a Monomythic Journey.

The journey, while prompted by feelings of discomfort, is always initiated with a purpose in mind. There is a problem or something missing in the hero's life or the life of their family or tribe, which is the source of the discomfort and for which there is no handy solution. The hero must journey to an oracle for an answer or to a strange land to retrieve a treasure. A loathly creature may announce the need for the journey and in some instances even provide the hero with a Magic Amulet for protection. .

In some myths, there is a drastic stripping away of all the supports of the hero. Odysseus, for example, starts with many ships and retainers but after several adventures and misadventures, he is left to face his trials alone. In keeping with the solitary impact of any psychological trauma, on his own he confronts the challenge, assisted only by his inner resources. Through some maneuver or other, the hero finds a way past seemingly impossible barriers until he or she breaks free. The hero retrieves a 'boon'. It may be a strategy to right a wrong, an answer to solve a question or a solution to whatever need prompted the quest. The hero returns from the journey with the boon in hand to set his or her world right.

There are thousands of variations of the hero myth. Some follow the full path from start to finish. Others stress only certain aspects or components of the adventure. Many reveal dangerous by-ways to be avoided. Many illustrate failure. Different aspects in different myths receive different emphases based on the original storyteller's unique intention and experience. The variations are myriad, but Campbell illustrates how they all follow the Monomythic pattern.

To summarize the process, the initiatory feeling that sets a personal quest in motion can be a problem or crisis, or even just discontent with the way things are. Restlessness in the face of a problem is the core feeling that initiates the hero's adventure. The hero descends into the belly of the whale and, like a captive in a mythological cooking pot, he or she simmers. Trials are encountered and overcome. A new perspective is acquired; a boon retrieved; and as the discomfort is dispelled, elation abounds. This is the core emotional pattern underlying the adventures of the heroes of mythology, and of the protagonists in classic fairy tales, and as we have seen, it is the emotional pattern within the creative act. As an imagistic equivalent of the revelatory or creative experience, the Monomyth's recurrence throughout the stories of mythology makes it a resource we can use consciously to become familiar with our innate creative talent.

As I've said, my personal revelatory experience was so chaotic that I was not really aware of what was happening to me. The myths I was reading for clues offered me only disjointed tidbits that seemed promising. It was only when I found Campbell's examination of the Monomyth that I was able to logically see the reality of what was happening to me. From the distilled experiences of thousands upon thousands of individuals from the past, the various aspects of my inspirational experience emerged clearly and in elaborate detail. By empathizing with the characters of the mythic tales, I lived their experiences vicariously in the reality of human emotional response. As a result, I was able to expand my knowledge and understanding of the creative act far beyond the boundaries of personal experience. In the chapters yet to come in this book, I will describe the main elements of the Monomythic Journey as I have lived it. I will introduce these key components by name and brief description to provide an overview of the principal strands that can be seen woven through any one monomythic story or life event.

My explorations of mythology led me to learn why creativity seems to be a rarity in the adult world: socialized mindsets easily keep us in tunnel-vision mode. Among such internalized restrictive responses, I discovered a major barrier to creativity arising out of the habit-forming function of the human mind. I call this "Mythlock" because it is hard to see new possibilities when your existing perspective blinds you to critical information. Scapegoatism is another barrier, an instinctual response that hijacks the discomforting emotional harbingers of the Monomythic adventure and vents them through anger upon any handy external entity. In this reflex, anger smothers creativity, just as in my account earlier of my reaction to being stumped by a simple math problem. Not until my anger passed and calm returned was my mind free to instigate my eureka moment. The rage of Scapegoatism not only inhibits creativity, but it is also the source of such horrific events as domestic violence and even genocide. Daily newspapers are full of the tragedy of Scapegoatism.

Another key mythical concept is the "Threshold Guardians". These figures are always present to prevent the timid from venturing into the unknown. We will explore their full role in the next section of this book, along with the importance of Magic Amulets in providing confidence for the hero to face the psychological challenges of the adventure. Self-confidence is essential for success. We will also explore the Magic Amulets of mythology in providing rescue from despair through a mythic, 'Rescue from Without.' You'll learn the psychological reality that lies behind these mythological Magic Amulets.

Across the threshold of the Magic Door, lies the Garden of the Goddess. This is the region of supernatural wonder, the realm of the mind, a realm of all possibilities, a realm of the unfettered imagination. This is the source of human genius wherein we can find an understanding for the most difficult problems we could ever face or even imagine. This is a fluid place alive with feeling-generated images. We are all familiar with its power because it is the same treasury that brings us dreams and nightmares. It gives us magnificent visions as well as some of the most horrific and frightening dream experiences. I learned that an exquisite vision from this imaginative realm could in the flash of an eye be transformed by negative emotions into an image of hell.

The part of the mythic adventure where my life flashed before my eyes and cast doubt upon my existing understanding served another vital purpose as well. I learned that within the Garden, suppressed negative emotions like guilt, regret, or anger are unleashed and can transform the whole experience. The Looking Glass, symbolic of seeing ourselves clearly, invites us to confront our unleashed dark feelings for good reason: they must be faced for our adventure to succeed. Negative emotions must be groomed and brought to light in front of the Looking Glass to clear the way for a safe Adventure into the fluid realm of the mind. You will recall that once I had confronted my guilt, experienced the pain of those I had foolishly hurt, and come to grips with those unleashed feelings, my Adventure began in earnest. Our emotions must be groomed in preparation for the adventure because within the Garden of the Goddess, the realm of all possibilities, negative emotions breed monsters of the mind.

Within the emotionally fluid Garden, even the Goddess has many manifestations. There is the Hag, the product of negative feelings towards things new or foreign. In the Garden, the Goddess bestows upon us a new perspective, but if the solution emerges contrary to existing biases, we react negatively, and the Goddess becomes the Hag. It is the nature of the Goddess, because of the fluidity of our minds, to always promise more. She beckons and entices us to break free from our limitations and become all that we can be. But a negative attitude to the enticements of the Goddess can transform all the images of the Garden and even the Goddess herself. The Garden becomes no longer a place of promise, but a place of excess, and the Goddess becomes the Seductrice. No longer does she beckon us to fulfill our destiny, but she becomes a temptress leading us into sin and depravity. It is our feelings that determine the nature of the images we encounter and our responses to those images that make the adventure a good trip or a bad trip.

If we can avoid, neutralize, or render positive the negative feelings that manifest the Hag, the Seductrice, or other horrible guises of the Goddess, we can experience a Meeting with the Goddess in all her splendor. A direct encounter with the Goddess is that fulfilling moment in our adventure when we discover an answer that is so beautiful, so profound, so exactly right that it takes our breath away. The beauty of the answer equals the adequacy of the answer to meet the emotional needs of the quest. The greater the beauty, the more appropriate the solution. With beauty comes a certainty that the truth has finally been revealed. Ironically, within the ecstasy of an encounter with the Goddess in all her splendor and glory lies one of the most insidious psychological traps awaiting an unsuspecting adventurer. Out of the mesmerizing beauty of a meeting with the Goddess arises the perilous Illusion of Truth.

Within the Garden of the Goddess lies all the human heart could ever desire. Here is the source of solutions to any problem of adaptation that could ever arise. Within the Garden the mind is fluid and because of this, it is in the nature of the Goddess to always promise more. If an adventurer can escape an encounter with the Hag or Seductrice and even the mesmerizing full encounter with the Goddess in all her splendor, the reward may be an invitation toward the pathway to the ultimate experience that waits at the top of the Stairway to the Stars. This path offers both liberation from the myths of the mind and access to limitless possibilities of the ultimate perspective. This is the experience of becoming one with the universe. This is often referred to as Nirvana and is the ultimate goal of any Monomythic Journey. In some religious mythologies, this peak is described as, seeing the face of god.

While acquiring a gift from the Goddess, feeling the elation of a Meeting with the Goddess, or experiencing the ecstasy of an ascent up the Stairway to the Stars may mark the climax of the adventure, a hero's journey is not yet finished. The final and hardest phase remains, the Return. The Garden of the Goddess, this inner, fluid, imaginative, virtual world, while it has a psychological reality, it has no footing in the real world. The answer that the adventurer has discovered is equally imaginative and virtual. Taking this inner boon and giving it an outer reality is the Challenge of the Return. This is the challenge of making dreams come true and the phase of the hero's journey that makes the history books. The emotional inner trajectory of the hero's achievements within the Garden of the Goddess coupled with the equally emotional outer challenges of the Return creates the iconic contents of the Monomythic Journey.

The Creative act or Adaptive Response is the process that takes us beyond the boundaries of our existing knowledge and experience to the source of visions of how things could be. This is the birth process of new ideas. Within this experience is the source of the actions of the great men and women of our world and '... without the more spectacular exploratory dives of the creative individual, there would be no science and no art' (Koestler 181). And there would be no great philosophies or religions. History books are filled with stories of the accomplishments of great men and women. Their ideas, their actions, their deeds, and their accomplishments make up a large portion of the content of history. But seldom is there mention of the inspirational experience, which underpins these accomplishments. Little is known about their experience of inspiration or revelation. Mythic tales about the adventures of the hero fill this gap, as does modern science's recognition of the universal psychological value of mythology's fantastic images.

As I worked my way through Campbell's study of the Monomyth, I gained not only an understanding of the experience I was undergoing but also an in-depth understanding of the creative process. Using an empathetic approach to the mythic tales, I was able to go far beyond my limited experience. I experienced many 'eureka' moments. I learned that within the realm of the mind lay all that the human heart could ever desire. I also learned that the measure of a truly successful Monomythic Journey is contained in the words of the fairy tale, 'and they lived happily ever after'. This is the goal of the Monomythic Journey. This is the ultimate reward of the creative life.

Campbell's Monomyth delineates the standard path of the mythic hero's adventure. It is a mythic equivalent of the creative act, which is a natural human response to a challenge of adaptation. This is the strategy we use, or which is thrust upon us when the solution to a crisis lies beyond the capability of our existing knowledge and experience to resolve. It is a critical human survival strategy that has transformed lives and continues to do so. Studying Campbell's Monomyth, I discovered an order underlying the chaos of my experience. Although there can be Monomyths within Monomyths and the adventure is never purely linear, it provides a logical path for an in-depth exploration of the Adaptive Response. I have used the Monomythic pattern as the organizing principle for this book. The goal is to take you on a Monomythic Journey, to make you familiar with the pattern, and hopefully to provide you with a new perspective on your own experiences. You will see that genius is not an inherited trait bestowed upon some and denied others, but merely a habit of mind and emotion. You will also come to realize that each of us is the hero – and the author -- of our own life story.

The Magic Door

If we change what we believe,
we change what we perceive.

Opening The Magic Door is the first step on the Monomythic Journey. We can explore some of its psychological aspects by looking at the details of the 'Eureka Phenomenon'. When Archimedes' boss first asked him to determine if his new crown was pure gold, the renowned scientist had no idea how to do so without destroying the crown. But days later, while lowering himself into his bath, he noticed, in an entirely new way, something he'd often seen before. Thanks to an unexpected new perspective, the solution suddenly popped into his mind. As a genius, Archimedes knew a solution existed and was confident that he could find it. Such confidence turns out to be a key to the opening of the Magic Door for any of us.

As observed earlier in detail, my youthful eureka experience with a math problem followed a similar pattern: I racked my brain until frustration turned to anger. Later, when I looked again in a calmer state, I saw the problem in a new light. I saw the problem from a new perspective. Like Archimedes, I was confident, not because I am a genius but because I knew that no teacher would assign an unsolvable math problem as homework. Like Archimedes, I tried in vain to solve the problem consciously until frustration turned to anger when success eluded me. Opening the Magic Door is an action of our unconscious minds, and conscious struggle and anger only hinder its functioning. Most importantly the gift from the Goddess is not an answer but a new perspective that reveals new information allowing our conscious minds to create an understanding.

This brief review of the Eureka Phenomenon demonstrates that if the problem is not a simple one with a simple answer, conscious thought cannot produce a solution when we lack adequate knowledge or experience. Frustration aroused by fruitless racking of the intellect alone inhibits the unconscious thought process, and anger slams the door. Confidence in ourselves to solve the problem and the belief that a solution exists provide the impetus for the unconscious mind to continue the search for a solution. And, most importantly, the gift of a trip beyond the Magic Door is a new perspective.

The "Eureka Phenomenon" is a powerful mini-variant of the Monomythic Journey. In this case, the Magic Door opens in a flash, casting new light on the problem, and closes immediately after. But most Monomythic Journeys involve a step across the threshold of the Magic Door into the wildly fluid realm of the human mind. People are fundamentally changed by the inspirational varieties of the revelatory experience. Many examples are found in Ovid's Metamorphoses, a whole collection of myths describing a variety of transformational impacts arising from the revelatory experience. The one critical element common to them all is a change of perspective when a hero transcends their perceptual box. This is the moment when the scales fall from our eyes, and everything is cast in a new light. This is the mind-altering moment symbolized by a Meeting with the Goddess.

The implications of this experience, if you give it a moment's thought, are extraordinary. The meaning we perceive in the world is shaped by the way we look at it rather than by any objective property of its own. This is not to say that there isn't an objective reality. Close your eyes and walk into a tree to meet objective reality. Yet our only access to understanding this reality is through personal perception founded on the meaning we give to the raw data of our senses. A closer understanding of the act of perception, upon which our understanding of reality is based, can provide us with a powerful adaptive advantage.

So the meaning we perceive is shaped by who we are, how we feel, and what we know and believe. It is shaped by the repertoire of knowledge and experience residing within our minds. In the words of Marshall McLuhan, 'We become what we behold, and we behold what we've become.' In the words of William Blake:

> If Perceptive Organs vary, Objects of
> Perception seem to vary:
> If Perceptive Organs close, their Objects
> seem to close also. (Blake 471)

If we change our minds, we can change our worlds. This is a reality of human perception.

Look at the familiar picture below: if we view the picture emphasizing the black areas on the sides, we see faces; if we look at it with the central white area in focus, we see a vase. Change your perspective and you can feel the inner re-orientation taking place within your mind.

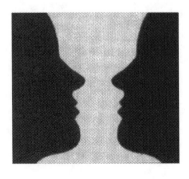

Although it is explained as an adjustment of foreground and background, we can sense that, through a mental adjustment or altering of perspective, we control the meaning of the picture. The picture below is of a stairway or a cornice. Since we do not spend a lot of our time staring at cornices, this visual switch can be more difficult. The stairway is clear because a stairway is familiar. The cornice is not as familiar.

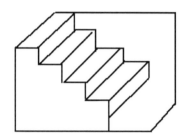

Of course, the cornice in this picture is a little more elaborate than those found in most houses. Imagine the top upper right corner as in the foreground, then look down and back to the left lower corner. Imagine stepping underneath the cornice. By the way, if you experience some frustration and even a slight elation when the cornice is finally viewed, you have a taste of the emotions of an inspirational process. Flip back and forth between the stairway and the cornice to feel the inner mental re-orientation that takes place. In both pictures, if we look at them one way, we see one meaning, if we look at them another way, we see another meaning. We determine meaning based on perspective.

Whether we see "faces" or "a vase", the reality is merely black-and-white areas separated by wiggly lines on the paper. Whether we see a "stairway'" or a "cornice", the reality is merely a series of straight lines on the paper. During the act of perception, the sensory data is organized within the mind, using our existing knowledge and experience, into a meaningful picture. All that ever reaches our mind from the external world is the raw data of our five senses. Light, with all its colors, is merely light of different wavelengths caught by the lens of the eye. Smell is the result of odorous chemical molecules attaching themselves to one of the thousands of receptors in our nose. Touch is the result of different pressures on touch-sensitive receptors in the skin. Baskin-Robbin's fifty-one ice cream flavors are combinations of only four basic tastes, sweet, sour, salty, and bitter, and all the noise and music we hear consists merely of vibrations in the air bouncing off the drums of our ears. During the act of perception, this raw sensory data is ordered to create meaning. If we alter the way we order this data, we alter the meaning we perceive.

The mental patterns we spontaneously apply are more than just static filters. They are patterns of experience. For example, take the meaning inherent in the word "day"' You can't see a "day." You can imagine the sun peeking its head above the eastern horizon, gradually rising to its zenith, and eventually sinking slowly into the west casting a red glow upon the lingering clouds. The concept or perceptual filter inherent in the word 'day' covers the whole procession of singular events creating meaning for the entire entity. Patterns covering processes are like small, short stories or mythic tales. Specific reality-based contents, like your previous experience of a sunrise and a sunset, become the contents of your understanding of a 'day'. The concept contained within the idea of a 'day' is used to order the contents of a sunrise and a sunset into a single meaningful perception. It is the understanding residing in our mind that creates meaning out of the raw data of our senses.

The dictionary definitions of perception reveal additional aspects, for example:

> Perception is the "name given to the mental process which refers sensations to an object [or event] which is recognized as identical [or closely related with one which has previously aroused similar sensations."(Universal Dictionary 848)

This definition stresses the fact that sensations or feelings play a role in the act of perception. Sensations, feelings, our emotions are involved during the act of perception as we try to relate a new object, event, or idea to our own experience that aroused similar feelings in the past. This is how we tap our repertoire of knowledge and experience to interact with the world. In any given situation, our feelings are the sensors we use to take stock. The feelings aroused in a given situation call to mind past events from our repertoire of knowledge and experience that have similar emotional coloring. This recalled knowledge creates an understanding of the new situation, or at least one close enough, allowing us to understand and act or react appropriately. These recalled ideas or beliefs are the short stories or myths of our minds that create meaning out of the raw data of our senses. In this way, our feelings select the myths or perceptual patterns we use to create meaning in any situation.

This role of our feelings in the act of perception is hard to recognize. It is a habitual process that happens so fast and most of the time without any particular feeling dominating at that time. But there are a couple of instances where the role of feelings in the act of perception is clear. One is when we encounter something we do not understand. This causes discomfort. The other case arises when, after struggling to understand, suddenly we see and understand. This is the elation of discovery. The intensity of the elation, once a new understanding is created, is directly proportional to the intensity of the discomfort that one is escaping.

The crisis I experienced when my girlfriend walked out on me caused depression. Life lost its meaning. As if in sympathy, the whole world that I observed was equally depressing and without meaning. In literature, they call this 'pathetic fallacy'. This occurs when, for example, the hero dies and suddenly the sky turns dark and ominous, and the rain begins to fall. It's called a fallacy because the real world has not changed. It's called 'pathetic', not because it is a cheap literary trick, but because it relates to the word 'empathy'. The literary device of 'pathetic fallacy' is reflective of an emotional/mental reality. When the hero dies, hope is lost. When I lost my girlfriend, I was locked into a depressing perspective that colored my whole world. It was as if images contrary to the way I was feeling were filtered out so that everything I saw was bleak.

But then as if by magic, at the moment of inspiration, I broke out of the box, acquired a new way of looking at things, and everything changed. The joy and ecstasy were unforgettable. One moment I was looking and seeing one thing, the next I was looking at the same thing, but all the meaning had changed. Everything was fresh and new. No wonder an epiphany is often described as being reborn. We become like children seeing the world anew.

As my life flashed before my eyes, I became aware that some of the conceptions I used to perceive the world were, in fact, misconceptions. Some of the myths that I lived by needed debunking. The inspirational moment, by creating a new perspective, can debunk those myths no longer adequate to the challenges at hand. Think about the implications of the fact that all the meaning we perceive is a product of the myths of our minds. If we change the myth, we change the meaning. If we change what we believe, we change what we perceive.

Every time I contemplate this reality I am blown away by the implications. Do you realize that, if everyone were aware of this fact of perception, suicide could become a thing of the past? If we knew that a mythic filter of our mind was the source of the depressing world we saw, we could change the myth and transform our world. Sadly, it is never as easy to do as it is to say, as we shall explore in the rest of this book. A new perspective emerges from a dynamically creative act, and passing through the Magic Door is the first step of any creative experience.

While the perceptual implications of a wild revelatory event are astounding, the simple reality underlying this experience is the truly remarkable fact that we hold the power of change. In Christian mythology, there is a verse that describes this aspect of perception.

> Your eye is the lamp of your body. When your eyes are good, your whole body also is full of light. But when they are bad, your body also is full of darkness. See to it, then, that the light within you is not darkness. Therefore, if your whole body is full of light, and no part of it is dark, it will be completely lighted. (Matthew 6:22-23 and Luke 11:34-36)

The choice is ours. Whether we see darkness and destruction, or wonder and awe, depends upon how we feel, and what we know and believe.

The Magic Door is the entranceway to the Monomythic Journey. The real adventure lies beyond the Magic Door where old and limiting ways of looking at things can be shattered and replaced with broader more comprehensive visions of the world. This is the realm of the human mind, a realm of endless possibilities, where emotions rule the landscape. Within mythology, this realm is called the World's Navel. And the world of Mythology is replete with images trying to express the limitless power of this realm:

> The torrent pours from an invisible source, the point of entry being the center of the symbolic circle of the universe, the Immovable Spot of the Buddha legend, around which the world may be said to revolve. Beneath this spot is the earth-supporting head of the cosmic serpent, the dragon, symbolic of the waters of the abyss, which are the divine life-creative energy and substance of the demiurge, the world-generating aspect of immortal being. The tree of life, i.e. the universe itself, grows from this point. It is rooted in the supporting darkness; the golden sun bird perches on its peak; a spring, the inexhaustible well, bubbles at its foot. Or the figure may be that of a cosmic mountain, with the city of the gods, like a lotus light, upon its summit, and in its hollow the cities of demons, illuminated by precious stones. Again, the figure may be that of the cosmic man or woman (for example the Buddha himself, or the dancing Hindu goddess Kali) seated or standing on this spot, or even fixed to a tree (Attis, Jesus, Wotan): ... the navel of the world, the umbilical point through which the energies of eternity break into time. Thus the World Navel is the symbol of continuous creation: the mystery of the maintenance of the world through that continuous miracle of vivification which wells within all things. (Campbell 40-41)

The World Navel lies at the center and is the source of 'continuous creation'. Imagine standing on a high hill and looking around. We see the sky touching the earth on every side. All around us stretches the horizon. Symbolically within the realm of our mind, each of us stands at the center of our universe and the horizon is the limit of our vision. Our horizon is circumscribed by the limits of our understanding, by the myths of our minds. We are each the center and the circumference of our own universe. We each are our own world's navel.

As discussed earlier, each of us possesses a repertoire of knowledge and experience built up over a lifetime. This resource creates the world that we perceive through the raw data of our senses. It consists of ideas and concepts imprinted emotionally in our minds and becomes the unconscious knowledge that guides us in life and, to some extent, represents who we are. Its purpose is to facilitate our adaptation to the world around us. However, the goal of life is the creation of a wonderful, happy life for ourselves and those around us. In the terminology of the fairy tale, we strive to 'live happily ever after'. Here is the criterion that determines the adequacy of the myths of our mind.

If happiness eludes us most of the time, we're ripe for a Monomythic Journey. The first step is to face how our existing fixed beliefs, the mind myths instilled in us so far, prevent that deep sense of well-being. When we are persistently unhappy, it is almost guaranteed that our fixed thoughts are busy quietly filtering out any new thoughts relevant to our potential joie de vivre. This insight is the essential first dramatic event of any inspirational experience. Once our blinders vanish, the creative process opens our perceptions in remarkable ways, and the Monomythic Journey leads us beyond our most stubborn limitations. Of course, knowledge of the potential rewards awakens and enriches our desire to step forth. The Monomythic

Journey is not only a way to discover a solution to a challenge; it is also a way to expand the horizons of our minds beyond our current limitations and beyond the limitations of our tribe.

The immediate reward of a Monomythic Adventure may be a simple solution to a simple problem or a dramatic insight into a troublesome mystery. But, as we will see, it is the nature of the Goddess to always promise more.

> The effect of the successful adventure of the hero
> is the unlocking and release again of the flow of
> life into the body of the world. (Campbell 40)

This is what awaits us when we step beyond the Magic Door. This is the potential of a Monomythic Journey.

Barriers to Creativity

Mythlock

We become what we behold, and
We behold what we've become.

Whenever we learn something, whether it is a complicated process or the simple naming of an object, we build an inner, mental concept that incorporates our understanding. We may play with the idea, test its validity, and modify it, if necessary until we are confident that our understanding is correct. Once this idea's reliability is proven and reinforced by successful use, it becomes habitual, without the need for our conscious attention. This is the learning process.

> We learn, or discover, with strenuous effort, a new method of thinking; after a while, with practice, the novelty changes into a semi-automatized routine ... and is incorporated into our repertory of habits. (Koestler 639)

This habit-forming function of the human mind is critical because if we had to be consciously aware of everything we did, we couldn't function. Watch a child learning to walk. They struggle; they fall; they try again and again until they get it right. As adults we don't even think about walking; we just do it. In fact, if we do think about it, we can become self-conscious and trip over our own two feet.

Once something is learned and becomes habitual, we no longer have to give it any thought, and our conscious minds are free to deal with more pressing concerns.

> ... we may regard this tendency towards the progressive automatization ... as an act of mental parsimony; as a handing-down of the controls to lower levels in the hierarchy of nervous functions, enabling the higher levels to turn to more challenging tasks. (Koestler 155)

In any situation we encounter, the feelings aroused select an existing concept from our repertoire of knowledge and experience to use during the act of perception. This concept or myth of the mind springs to the fore, creating an understanding for the raw sensory data arising in the situation so we know how to react appropriately, or occasionally inappropriately. This all transpires without conscious awareness.

There is a price that is paid for this mental parsimony. A large portion of the meaning we perceive arises from learned concepts of which we are no longer consciously aware.

> These silent codes can be regarded as condensations of learning into habit. Habits are the indispensable core of stability and ordered behavior; they also tend to become mechanized and reduce man to the status of a conditioned automaton. (Koestler 96)

We are creatures of habit, responding habitually in most of the situations we encounter. These silent codes are the invisible myths of our minds: we are unaware of their existence or their extensive impact on our perceptions. We determine the meaning we perceive based upon the existing myths of our individual mind, the engrained assumptions we bring to everything.

> We become what we behold, and
> We behold what we've become.

These mental myths also filter out sensory noise that appears irrelevant to the meaning they assume exists. The problem is that this filtered sensory data may contain information key to a more accurate or more useful understanding of the actual situation. Yet, we remain unaware of that screened-out data. These unconscious biases reframe the raw data of our senses and create the bars of our cage of Mythlock.

Most of our basic attitudes and key understandings are fixed as personal beliefs by middle childhood. It is reasonable to assume that some of the understandings created by an eight-year-old may be slightly off the mark. For example, a friend of mine mentioned that as a kid he remembered one line from the song Silent Night as 'Sleep in heavenly peas'. For years he sang the words 'Sleep in heavenly peas'. Finally, he gave it a moment's conscious attention and realized it couldn't be right. It wasn't. The line is actually 'Sleep in heavenly peace'. How much of the world we understand is filled with similar minor or even major misconceptions? We will never know, because we are creatures of habit who are unaware of the invisible myths of our minds busily creating the meaning that we perceive. We are also unaware that these ingrained personal biases filter out as "irrelevant" any information contrary to the meaning they create.

For example, I had a discussion with my sister-in-law some time ago in which she described a situation she observed frequently at conferences. Although I attend many conferences, I had never seen what she was describing, and I told her so.

A couple of months later, at a conference, I was listening politely, like everyone else, to a man presenting an ill-prepared presentation filled with clichés and absolutely nothing new. After him came a woman with a well-organized presentation filled with valuable ideas, I could take home and use in my department. I looked around and my jaw dropped. I saw what my sister-in-law had described. Four separate groups of men were carrying on discussions at the same time the woman was talking. I saw no groups like that when the man was talking. I was witnessing something I'd not noticed before – culturally unconscious, ingrained discriminatory behavior of men towards women. To make matters worse, I immediately started a fifth group of men talking about my new eye-opening discovery. How much more is going on in our worlds that we are simply not noticing because of the blinding impact of the invisible myths of our minds?

It is not easy to undo these 'faulty integrations', the invisible myths affecting our cognition, for two reasons. First, because we are unaware of their existence, and second, because of the insidious nature of these myths themselves. They not only create the meaning we perceive; they also filter out information irrelevant to the meaning their biases create.

> To undo wrong connections, faulty integrations,
> is half the game. To acquire a new habit is easy
> because one main function of the nervous system
> is to act as a habit-forming machine; to break out
> of a habit is an almost heroic feat of mind and
> character. (Koestler 190)

Look back at the picture of the faces and the vase (Page 36-37). Note that it is impossible to see both the faces and the vase at the same time. Now imagine for a minute that you were totally unaware that seeing a vase was even a possibility. All you would see would be the two faces in the picture. The other possibility would remain hidden.

> The abstracting and recording of information involves ... the sacrifice of details which are filtered out as irrelevant in a given context. But what is considered as irrelevant in one context, may be relevant in another. (Koestler 518)

We are surrounded by sensory noise, but our perceptual organs protect us by filtering out the irrelevant. If some of this information is relevant to the reality of the situation, it is still filtered out. This is the trap of Mythlock.

Many mythic stories and folktales portray how Mythlock shapes actions and their consequences. The scholar Aurelio Espinosa (1880-1958) cataloged two hundred and sixty-seven versions of this genre from around the world (Espinosa 129-209). They are called the tar-baby stories. Following is an Uncle Remus sanitized version of the common folktale:

> One day after Brer Rabbit had fooled him with the calamus root, Brer Fox set up a tar-baby in the middle of the road, and then he hid in the bushes to see what would happen. He didn't wait very long, for by and by there came Brer Rabbit pacing down the road. When he came upon the tar-baby, he stood on his hind legs very much astonished. "Good morning!" said Brer Rabbit. "Nice weather this morning!" Tar-Baby made no reply. "Are you deaf?" said Brer Rabbit. "If you are I can holler louder." Tar-baby kept still and Brer Rabbit said, "You are stuck up, that is what you are. And I am going to cure you. I am going to teach you to talk to respectable people if it

is the last thing I do. If you don't take off your hat and tell me 'How do you do' I am going to kill you."

Brer Rabbit kept on asking and the tar-baby made no reply. Finally he raised his fist and struck tar-baby on the side of the head. It stuck. "If you don't let me loose I'll knock you again," said Brer Rabbit, and saying this he struck with his other hand, and that stuck also. "Turn me loose or I'll knock the stuffing out of you," said Brer Rabbit, and he struck with his feet and they also stuck. Then he cried to the tar-baby to let him go otherwise he would butt him with his head. And he butted and his head stuck.

At that moment Brer Fox came out and laughed and laughed until he could laugh no more. He went then to prepare the fire to roast Brer Rabbit. (Espinosa, p. 174-5)

Brer rabbit is trapped, stuck to the tar-baby in five places (i.e. five senses), and the more he thrashes about the more stuck he becomes. To soften the potential horror of the story, the Uncle Remus version lets Brer Rabbit trick the fox and escape into the briar patch. But there are versions where the character is caught, killed, eaten, or forced to suffer some other indignity. The tar-baby stories from folklore and mythology are descriptions of the psychological reality of Mythlock.

The fact that Mythlock is such a dominant feature of human endeavors has given rise to another worldwide genre of mythic tales. These are the stories of the trickster gods. Because we interact so habitually with the world around us, forgetting that all the meaning we perceive is a product of our minds, the trickster gods of mythology have a field day with our naiveté. The story about the West African trickster-divinity Edshu is just one example of how human beings can be tricked because we forget that the meaning we perceive is a product of our minds and not a fixed property of the external world.

> One day, this odd god came walking along a path between two fields. He beheld in either field a farmer at work and proposed to play the two a turn. He donned a hat that was on one side red but on the other white, green before and black behind; …so that when the two friendly farmers had gone home to their village and the one had said to the other, 'Did you see that old fellow go by today in the white hat?' the other replied. 'Why, the hat was red.' To which the first retorted, 'It was not; it was white.' 'But it was red,' insisted the friend, 'I saw it with my own two eyes.' 'Well you must be blind,' declared the first. 'You must be drunk,' rejoined the other. And so the argument developed and the two came to blows. (Campbell 45)

Think of the many arguments you've witnessed, perhaps including your own, in which the topic was familiar to both participants, yet each saw it from a different perspective and gave it an entirely different 'meaning'. Unsurprisingly, police officers are alert to this aspect of human perception. A car proceeding down a street hits a pedestrian. One witness, a pedestrian, describes the event to the officer. "The car came careening down the street swerved, and hit the poor pedestrian trying to cross the street." By contrast, another witness, a young, eager driver describes the event, saying, "The car was coming down the street when suddenly that idiot stepped right out in front of it and the driver swerved to avoid him." The same incident, the same situation, but two entirely different meanings based upon the invisible myths of the mind.

It is not only trickster gods of mythology who have a field day with this reality of human perception; it provides the raw material for humor every day. Particular fun can be made of those who believe they can be objective and entirely free from the coloring filters of the myths of their minds.

> 'One may say broadly', Bertrand Russell wrote in 1927, 'that all animals that have been carefully observed have behaved so as to confirm the philosophy in which the observer believed before his observations began. Nay, more, they have all displayed the national characteristics of the observer. Animals studied by Americans rush about frantically, with an incredible display of hustle and pep, and at last achieve the desired result by chance. Animals observed by Germans sit still and think, and at last evolve the situation out of their inner consciousness. (Koestler 556.)

We all view our world through the veil of Mythlock. If confronted with a new challenge or crisis in our lives, although a solution may stand right in front of our noses, it can be hidden by the myths of our minds. We forget that all meaning is a product of our minds when we mistakenly believe that it is an objective property of the external world.

There is a classic myth that symbolically represents a successful escape from Mythlock. It is one of the earliest examples of the tar-baby motif although, rather than a tar-baby, it tells of a sticky-haired monster. It's called the myth of Prince Five-Weapons. In this version of the story, Prince Five Weapons is aware of the nature of Mythlock. He knows that if all else fails, if his knowledge, weapons, and even his five senses fail him, a strategy to escape lies within.

It is told of a young prince who had just completed his military studies under a world-renowned teacher. Having received, as a symbol of his distinction, the title 'Prince Five-Weapons,' he accepted the five weapons that his teacher gave him, bowed and, armed with the new weapons, struck out onto the road leading to the city of his father, the king. On the way he came to a certain forest. People at the mouth of the forest warned him. "Sir Prince, do not enter this forest," they said; "an ogre lives here, named Sticky-hair; he kills every man he sees."

But the prince was confident and fearless as a maned lion. He entered the forest just the same. When he reached the heart of it, the ogre showed himself. The ogre had increased his stature to the height of a palm tree; he had created for himself a head as big as a summer house with bell-shaped pinnacle, eyes as big as alms bowls, two tusks as big as giant bulbs or buds; he had the beak of a hawk; his belly was covered with blotches; his hands and feet were dark green. "Where are you going?" he demanded. "Halt! You are my prey!"

Prince Five-Weapons answered without fear, but with great confidence in the arts and crafts that he had learned. "Ogre," said he, "I knew what I was about when I entered this forest. You would do well to be careful about attacking me; for with an arrow steeped in poison will I pierce your flesh and fell you on the spot!"

Having thus threatened the ogre, the young prince fitted to his bow an arrow steeped in deadly poison and let fly. It stuck right in the ogre's hair. Then he let fly, one after another, fifty arrows. All stuck right to the ogre's hair. The ogre shook off every one of those arrows, letting them fall right at his feet, and approached the young prince.

Prince Five-Weapons threatened the ogre a second time, and drawing his sword, delivered a masterly blow. The sword, thirty-three inches long, stuck right in the ogre's hair. Then the prince smote him with a spear. That also stuck right in his hair. Perceiving that the spear had stuck, he smote him with a club. That also stuck right in his hair.

When he saw that the club had stuck, he said: "Master ogre, you have never heard of me before. I am Prince Five-Weapons. When I entered this forest infested by you, I took no account of bows, and suchlike weapons; when I entered this forest, I took account only of myself. Now I am going to beat you and pound you into powder and dust!" Having thus made known his determination, with a yell he struck the ogre with his right hand. His hand stuck right to the ogre's hair. He struck him with his left hand. That also stuck. He struck him with his right foot. That also stuck. He struck him with his left foot. That also stuck. Thought he: "I will beat you with my head and pound you into powder and dust!" He struck him with his head. That also stuck right to the ogre's hair.

Prince Five-Weapons, snared five times, stuck fast in five places, dangled from the ogre's body. But for all that, he was unafraid, undaunted. As for the ogre, he thought: "This is some lion of a man, some man of noble birth -- no mere man! For although he has been caught by an ogre like me, he appears neither to tremble nor to quake! In all the time I have harried this road, I have never seen a single man to match him! Why, pray, is he not afraid?" Not daring to eat him, he asked: "Youth, why are you not afraid? Why are you not terrified with the fear of death?"

"Ogre, why should I be afraid? For in one life, one death is absolute certain. What's more, I have in my belly a thunderbolt for a weapon. If you eat me, you will not be able to digest that weapon. It will tear your insides into tatters and fragments and will kill you. In that case, we'll both perish. That's why I'm not afraid!"

"What this youth says is true," thought the ogre, terrified with the fear of death. "From the body of this lion of a man, my stomach would not be able to digest a fragment of flesh even so small as a kidney bean. I'll let him go!" And he let Prince Five-Weapons go. The Future Buddha preached the Doctrine to him, subdued him, made him self-denying, and then transformed him into a spirit entitled to receive offerings in the forest. Having admonished the ogre to be heedful, the youth departed from the forest, and at the mouth of the forest told his story to human beings; then went his way. (Campbell 85-88)

When first confronted by the challenge of the ogre, the Prince unleashes arrows, then his sword, then his spear, followed by his club. The Prince uses all his weapons, knowledge, and skills to attempt to defeat the Sticky-Haired Ogre. When that fails, he hits the ogre with his right hand, then his left, then his right foot, then his left, and finally he butts him with his head. Five times he strikes the ogre and each time he becomes stuck. He uses his five senses to analyze the situation, but this strategy fails. The raw data of his senses do not provide the information he requires to escape from the Sticky-Haired Ogre because the raw data of his senses is filtered out of the relevant information by the existing myths of his mind. Not until he calls upon the thunderbolt within is he able to escape. In myth, the thunderbolt is a major symbol signifying the power of enlightenment, which shatters the illusory realities of the world (Campbell 87). When caught in the cage of Mythlock, all the Prince's knowledge, experience, and weapons are rendered useless. Only when he dives into the untapped resources of his mind and finds a new way of looking at things is he able to determine a solution to his dilemma.

The myth of Prince Five-Weapons tells of an escape from Mythlock by one who is aware of the nature of his conditioned bias. He is as nimble-minded as he is courageous. However, for most of us, the invisible myths of our minds operate without our conscious awareness, so we tend to forget that all meaning is a product of our minds.

As a result, Mythlock infests our world and is reflected again and again in human endeavors. A most glaring example of Mythlock, in our current age, is the "Big Lie" of Donald Trump, past president of the U.S. Even before the 2020 presidential election was over, he started spreading the lie that his 'victory' was being stolen from him by the opposing party. His followers believed him, and it became their truth. The lie persists; today it seems that the majority of the republican party in the U.S. believe it, despite countless unsuccessful lawsuits showing it to be false. It led to the now infamous January 6th, 2021 attack on the U.S. Capital. In spite of all the information revealed about the incident, a significant number of Republicans believe that the January 6th assault was a patriotic effort to preserve democracy in the U.S.

A much more dangerous case of Mythlock currently infects all the cultures of the world. The increase of carbon dioxide in the air arising from the harvesting and burning of fossil fuels is changing the atmosphere of the entire world. The increased heat is causing droughts, and now the summer news is filled with the disaster of wildfires sweeping through our forests, increasing in frequency and violence every year. The increasing amount of water rising into our air from the evaporation of the oceans is falling not in a gentle rain but as rivers of rain, causing devastating floods, their frequency and violence ever increasing. Naturally, those whose lives depend upon the harvesting of fossil fuels see Global Warming as a manufactured attack upon their lifestyle and fight back, funded by the enormous wealth of the fossil fuel industry. The number of species going extinct is also increasing and, if this man-made potential disaster continues, it could result in the extinction of all the animal species of the world, including mankind.

The fact remains that we all inhabit our own cage of Mythlock. What emotions arise when we are caught in its sticky tar? My homework struggle with the sticky math problem springs to mind again. I looked at the problem this way, that way, every conceivable way, but no matter how much I thrashed about, the answer eluded me. Extreme frustration that grew into anger dominated the ordeal. The simple answer that lay right in front of my eyes was effectively invisible. My five senses failed me because any information that might have helped was filtered out as irrelevant by my existing perspective, and my anger totally slammed the door on the process. Until I calmed down, stepped back, and unconsciously acquired a new perspective, the solution remained hidden. The only positive way out is the creative act. Until our perspective changes, the solution remains hidden, and anger slams the door. The creative act, the adaptive response, offers us Escape from Mythlock.

Scapegoatism

Scapegoatism hijacks the discomforting emotions of the creative act and vents them through anger upon any innocent external entity.

'Think out of the box!' This well-known success mantra encourages us to stretch toward our goals in innovative ways. The "box" referred to here is precisely the cage of Mythlock.

Ironically, what arises out of the learning process becomes, in time, a barrier rather than an aid to creativity. Our accumulated knowledge, both a key to stability and an essential resource for our survival, tends, over time, because of the habit-forming nature of learning, to turn us into automatons. We become puppets yanked about by the strings of the invisible myths of our minds. All is well until we encounter an adaptive challenge beyond the scope of our existing understanding, which is the current condition in our rapidly evolving world. Then the blinding effect of Mythlock becomes a major reason for the rarity of creative genius.

There is another equally strong barrier that is not learned. It is a built-in, instinctual response designed solely for survival. It is a critical survival strategy, but when misapplied in a situation of adaptation, it becomes yet another barrier to creativity. I experienced this instinctual response, one summer when I was just eleven years old and my family was vacationing at my grandfather's cottage. It was a warm summer day and I had spent the afternoon wandering the beach, collecting stones, shells, and weird-shaped pieces of driftwood. Before I knew it, the afternoon was gone; by the time I got home, supper was over. More disturbing than the loss of supper was the news that my sisters had gone to the drive-in movie without me. There was no way this kid was going to spend an evening at home with the adults when his sisters were at the drive-in theatre only a couple of miles down the road. So, off I went to join them.

The drive-in was down a gravel road through a scrub bush. It was dark. The clear sky was filled with stars, but there was no moon. Soon the cottage lights faded behind me, and darkness closed in. I had covered about three-quarters of a mile when I saw him. There in the bushes was a dark figure puffing on a cigarette and then cupping his hand to hide the glow. He wasn't alone; there were others with him. I quickened my pace, but they kept even with me, creeping along through the bushes. A twig snapped and I panicked and ran. I swear I set a record for the mile by an eleven-year-old! Although there are more benign explanations for what I saw that night than a clutch of gangsters out to kidnap me, my response, once I believed I had correctly identified the apparition as a source of danger, was instinctual. My response was flight.

This automatic human response to a threat is, of course, called the 'fight-or-flight response'. Whenever confronted with a potential threat to our safety, the first thing we do is scan the environment to identify the source of the problem so we can determine whether the best response is to fight or turn and run. Even startled by a loud noise, we automatically respond this way. Our ancient ancestors inhabited a dangerous world filled with larger and stronger animals. Being quick to respond to external danger was key to their survival. Although the lions are gone from most neighborhoods, it still remains a critical survival tool. Hearing a screech of tires in a public space, alerts us to seek the source so we can leap out of the path of the vehicle. Hearing a warning shout, we – from the corner of our eye -- can catch sight of the tree falling towards us and leap to safety. The response is instinctual, and its purpose is survival. Whether we identify the external source as something we can handle or something we can't, we are made adrenaline-ready for action. In this way, whenever we're alarmed, in a flash we're alert, tense, uncomfortable, and even fearful, while our bodies are immediately primed for action. This instinctual response happens all the time, even when there is no actual threat, as in my case of imagined gangsters hiding in the bushes.

I recall an event in which my response was fight rather than flight. It happened indoors in the middle of a winter night. Our furnace hadn't been turned down, so the air was warm and extremely dry. I woke up needing a glass of water. Quietly I crawled out from under the covers. Head down, I tiptoed across the room stepping carefully around my clothes and shoes scattered on the floor. Slowly my eyes began to adjust to the dark. Suddenly I sensed something right in front of me, and my head shot up, smashing my face right into the edge of a partially opened door. Alerted, I instantly identified the source of the threat as something that I could handle. I cursed and kicked the door with my bare foot. My fall to the floor, writhing in pain from the door's blow upon my soft fleshy toe, left the wisdom of my fighting response in question, but it did prove the lack of rational thought involved in this instinctual response.

Often, we simply fail to recognize our automatic actions as arising from a fight-or-flight response. We stub our toe on a chair and swear at the chair for being there. We absentmindedly lock our keys in the car and blame someone nearby for distracting us, causing our error. Oblivious to our stupidity, we react without conscious thought, unable to see our accusation as the absurdity it is. Fight-or-flight is meant to be a critical survival strategy, but we all have lived examples of its misapplication.

When the problem we face is not an external threat but an adaptive challenge, flight becomes difficult. Although it may be possible to run away from problems, when the problem is our own need to adapt to a changing world, flight is not possible. How do you run away from yourself? You can't. When an internal challenge triggers our wired-in fight-or-flight response, fight is the only available option. So, we project our anger outward, and as we vent it upon any handily-identified external source of the problem, our discomfort dissipates. We kick the door or shout at our partners. When I faced my crisis, I first blamed my girlfriend, then alcohol, then the whole damn capitalist system, then my parents, then religion, and finally god.

The urgent need of the conscious mind is to release pent-up uneasy feelings, and an eruption of anger works well. An instinctual response that would support survival from a threat of external danger becomes futile when there is no external peril. Our thoughtless submission to the fight-or-flight response is another primary reason for the rarity of creative genius. Instinctive misuse of the fight response is called Scapegoatism. Its consequences are dire.

At the core of the fight-or-flight response is a simple emotional pattern initiated by alarm and uneasiness. If we fight, the emotion of anger dispels our discomfort. If we flee, the emotion of panic does the same thing. By contrast, if there is no external threat, our uneasiness persists. With flight from non-existent danger impossible, our conscious mind lands on any handy external target to vent our shock and rage. Directed outward, these emotions feel much better than the inner weight of helpless angst. Unfortunately, when we choose a convenient target to blame, we are practicing scapegoatism.

It is natural that feelings of distress and restlessness arise when we face an adaptive challenge. These unpleasant emotions are intimations of a Monomythic Adventure's urgently prodding our minds towards inspiration and creative change. Unfortunately, they can be easily hijacked by the fight-or-flight response, leaving the problem unresolved. A change of perspective, not a mere rearrangement of the environment, is the route to a solution. However, we mistakenly tend to focus on a scapegoat instead of on an actual solution. Doing this, resolves nothing and may well unleash cultural violence on the world. As noted earlier in these pages, reactive anger slams the door on the creative experience, thus forestalling personal insight. Sad to say, history is littered with examples of the devastating outcomes of scapegoatism.

Let's reconsider one of history's most devastating examples of how extreme scapegoatism's damage can become. When the economic depression of the 1930s descended upon Europe, the challenge of adaptation was dropped into the laps of millions. Anxiety, despair, and helplessness dominated the emotions of the populace. In Germany, politicians guided troubled citizens to identify an external source of the problem within their midst. The authorities declared 'The Jews' to be responsible for the economic devastation ruining the nation. Here was a convenient external entity upon which to vent the growing social tensions. By designating a certain race of people to blame for economic and cultural chaos, Germany's leaders cleverly redirected the people's anger, purposely manipulating these emotions. This extreme policy of scapegoatism led to the murders of six million innocent Jews, gypsies, and other minorities during the Second World War.

The human race has not learned from that experience. Consider the fall of communism in Yugoslavia in the early 1990s: a disintegration of the political and economic systems throws the populace into confusion and chaos. Anxiety and despair, emotional precursors of the Adaptive Response, are vented through anger upon an identified external source of the problem. For the Serbs, the problem is the Croats. For the Croats, the problem is the Serbs. Bolstered by centuries of such tribal bickering, those in positions of power unleash a program of rape and genocide. We could assemble quite a list of such conflicts in the last 100 years.

Nothing has changed in our current world. Unrestricted capitalism has allowed CEOs to move their manufacturing to countries with low wages and return with phenomenally inexpensive goods and phenomenally high returns for their investors. Meanwhile, once thriving cities, where these goods were previously manufactured, are now inhabited by vacant, deteriorating factories, and the lives of thousands of families are disrupted. Many factories are still booming but filled with robots rather than human workers.

The degree of discomfort prompting an adaptive response depends upon the impact the changes are having on our lives. If we're subject to minor discomfort, we merely seek an understanding so we can stop thinking about it. If angst and worry are tearing us apart, the question seems to the brain more like a scream for help. The brain moves quickly to find a way to diminish the angst that is tearing us apart. It seems that any answer will do in a storm: for example, "It's the Jews, the blacks, the homos, or those immigrants stealing our jobs." Once again scapegoatism triumphs, the innocent suffer, and nothing is resolved.

Scapegoatism is insidious. To see it clearly, we have to identify the emotional pattern -- discomfort in a situation without immediate danger where the emotions of discomfort are vented through anger upon a handy external entity. For instance, I remember pacing back and forth in front of the windows of our house, peering out whenever I heard the sound of a car in the street. My daughter is late. One hour past curfew and still she isn't home. Another hour passes and images of car accidents sweep through my mind. My anxiety grows and worry builds. I start to imagine scenes of illicit sex, which my imagination expands to images of rape and murder. My imagination runs rampant, and the anxiety and worry grow until I hear a car in the driveway. My anxiety is immediately transformed into anger. I understand; I 'know' the source of the problem that caused this nightmare evening; I identify an external entity upon which to vent my anxiety through anger. I yell at my daughter; ground her for a month and banish her new boyfriend from our house forever. A Monomythic Adventure beckons me to come to grips with the unleashed power of my imagination, but this Monomythic Adventure is avoided through Scapegoatism.

I would be remiss if I didn't say something about the role of Mythlock and scapegoatism in our current crazy world. Although there continues to be an alarming incidence of mass murders even today in 2023, let us consider the mass shooting tragedy a decade ago in Sandy Hook, Connecticut, US as an example. On December 14, 2012, a 20-year-old male shot and killed 26 people including his mother. Twenty of his victims were children between six and seven years old (Wikipedia). Even now, my eyes fill with tears whenever I contemplate this violent event. Crying is the only way I can mitigate the pain. By contrast, an American talk show host named Alex Jones found another way to mitigate his horror: he found utter denial in calling the Sandy Hook attack a 'hoax' of the 'fake news' media. He claimed that the parents seen grieving their loss were merely actors, and he broadcast this lie to his social media audience.

Then the computer algorithms of social media took over. Anyone who listened to Jones or read something professing his lie started to receive on their own social media unsolicited article after article 'confirming' the lie. Anything counter to his lie was portrayed as just a product of the fake-news media. For anyone believing Alex Jones's lie, the discomfort of the tragedy was replaced by anger toward those presumably promoting the "hoax". In fact, some of the people blinded by the reinforced mythlock of that lie began attacking the bereaved parents.

In situations like the divergent reactions to Sandy Hook, we see mythlock and scapegoatism flourishing in our recent culture. In the current environment of rapid change and disruptive events, scapegoatism is ubiquitous. While newspaper images show us the bruised and battered faces of frightened women, a spouse murdered, a girlfriend killed, and children beaten, too few see what is behind these assaults, much less how to prevent them. Scapegoatism continues spreading like a latent virus within us all, standing ever-ready to infect our lives. Glaring is the failure of scapegoatism to produce an appropriate answer to whatever the issue may be.

Since scapegoatism hijacks the emotions of the adaptive response, its dynamic leaves us powerless to progress in positive ways. It invites us to believe that a solution always lies outside our control. It is pitiable that the vast untapped resources of the human mind, the creative potential within us capable of resolving problems, remains largely untapped. Where it is tapped, and solutions offered for discussion, mythlock blinds the majority of us to its promise, and scapegoatism threatens the messenger with violence. Inspiration and revelation through accepting the call of the Monomythic Journey can offer us solutions to life's most intractable problems. Sadly, the call to real change is too often bypassed by ingrained habits of mythlock and scapegoatism. Of course, ingrained scapegoatism is far from new among humankind's responses to difficulty. Both history and ancient folktales are replete with examples. For one, there is in the classical Greek pantheon a god named Pan, a figure who haunts the forests and meadows of the land. He has small goat horns poking out of his head, and hooves instead of feet. Pan can be a dangerous god. Joseph Cambell writes of him,

> The emotion that he instilled in human beings who by accident adventured into his domain was "panic" fear, a sudden groundless fright. Any trifling cause then -- the break of a twig, the flutter of a leaf – would flood the mind with imagined danger, and in the frantic effort to escape from his own aroused unconscious, the victim expired in a flight of dread. (Campbell 81)

During my terrified run to the drive-in theatre that long-ago night, I did not 'expire in a flight of dread,' but I certainly panicked. Had the story of Pan been a part of my childhood experience, I might have seen this strange apparition in the bushes as Pan and his cohorts out for an evening cigarette. I could have paid my respects and walked calmly on. Had I been more knowledgeable of the phenomena of the night, I might have understood the apparition as fireflies and enjoyed the spectacle. As it was, immersed in popular movies' criminal themes, I saw gangsters out to kidnap me, and I full-on panicked. Panic is not a reaction conducive to survival.

Embedded within the idea of a belief in Pan as representative of a force of nature around and within us, we glimpse a psychological strategy of the mythmakers. Pan was much more than merely a dreaded creature of the night. As a deity, writes Campbell,

> Pan was benign to those who paid him worship, yielding the boons of the divine hygiene of nature: bounty to the farmers, herders, and fisherfolk who dedicated their first fruits to him, and health to all who properly approached his shrines of healing. (Campbell 81)

If we avoid the inappropriate, instinctual, fight-or-flight response when confronted with an adaptive challenge, if we properly pause and approach Pan's shrines of healing, looking inward with humility; if we follow the path of the Adaptive Response, healing is our reward -- the healing of creative inspiration.

The emotions called up by an adaptive challenge can be excruciating: helplessness, depression, and despair can crush the human spirit. Yes, the anger of scapegoatism can distract us from despair, but it does nothing to resolve the actual issue. If we recognize these disruptive feelings as harbingers of a Monomythic Adventure, the way is open to genuine healing. Transformative inspiration is Pan's reward to us for daring the journey toward insight rather than bypassing it.

The barriers to creative genius are legion. Even if we can escape the trap of Mythlock and avoid the slippery slope of scapegoatism, there are still more barriers that can keep us from the revitalization of our lives, which is the reward that awaits us within the Garden of the Goddess.

Threshold Guardians

Within the Garden of the Goddess, fear breeds monsters of the mind.

Scapegoatism and Mythlock are two powerful reasons for the rarity of creative genius. Both stem from the natural workings of the human mind: mythlock is a function of perception wherein the myths of our minds hide information we need for successful adaptation. Scapegoatism, on the other hand, occurs when an instinctual human response to danger hijacks the emotions of discomfort and then vents them through anger upon an innocent external entity. There is another reason for the rarity of creative genius: it is avoidance. The simplest response to the emotional discomfort caused by any challenge of adaptation is to avoid it. But avoiding a challenge of adaptation has a high price. The price is a limitation of our horizons and a reduction of our potential. Failure to meet an adaptive challenge means an impoverishment of our lives.

There is a famous story of Apollo, the god of love, and Daphne, daughter of the River Peneus, which illustrates the emotional process of what is mythically known as a "refusal of the call" (Campbell 59). It clearly shows the restricting aftereffects of a refusal to face a challenge of adaptation. As the story goes, love comes to the beautiful maiden Daphne in the person of the god Apollo but when he approaches, she flees.

> "I who pursue thee am no enemy. Thou knowest not whom thou fleest, and for that reason dost thou flee. Run with less speed, I pray, and hold

thy flight. I, too, will follow with less speed. Nay, stop and ask who thy lover is."

"He would have said more," the story goes, "but the maiden pursued her frightened way and left him with words unfinished, even in her desertion seeming fair. The winds bared her limbs, the opposing breezes set her garments aflutter as she ran, and a light air flung her locks streaming behind her. Her beauty was enhanced by flight. But the chase drew to an end, for the youthful god would not longer waste his time in coaxing words, and, urged on by love, he pursued at utmost speed. Just as when a Gallic hound has seen a hare in the open plain, and seeks his prey on flying feet, but the hare, safety; he, just about fasten on her, now, even now, thinks he has her, and grazes her very heels with outstretched muzzle; but she knows not whether or not she be already caught, and barely escapes from those sharp fangs and leaves behind the jaws just closing on her: so ran the god and maid, he sped by hope and she by fear. But he ran the more swiftly, borne on the wings of love, gave her no time to rest, hung over her fleeing shoulders and breathed on the hair that streamed over her neck. Now was her strength all gone, and pale with fear and utterly overcome by the toil of her swift flight, seeing the waters of her father's river near, she cried: 'O father, help! If your waters hold divinity, change and destroy this beauty by which I pleased o'er well.' Scarce had she thus prayed when a down-dragging numbness seized her limbs, and her soft sides were begirt with thin bark. Her hair was changed to leaves, her arms to branches. Her feet, but now so swift, grew fast in sluggish roots, and her head was now but a tree's top. Her gleaming beauty alone remained.

This is indeed a dull and unrewarding finish, Apollo, the sun, the lord of time and ripeness, no longer pressed his frightening suit, but instead, simply named the laurel his favorite tree and ironically recommended its leaves to the fashioners of victory wreaths. The girl had retreated to the image of her parent and there found protection -- (Campbell 61-62)

Daphne in refusing to open herself to the adventure of love remains rooted in the past and misses an opportunity for one of life's great adventures.

From a radical feminist perspective, the interpretation of this myth is simple. If you are a beautiful woman, the world gives you three choices: make yourself ugly, drown yourself, or submit to rape. But if we examine the emotional core of this myth there is a broader, more profound interpretation that also applies equally to a male or female. Remember, mythic tales are externalized dreams. Every time love approaches, Daphne's fear of love arises, perhaps engendered in her as a child witnessing the brutality inflicted upon her mother by her father. Remember, within the world of dreams, fear breeds monsters of the mind. This time the monster is a vicious hound threatening to tear her apart. So, whenever love approaches Daphne, she rejects it and instead of a life filled with the joy of family, husband, kids, grandkids, etc., she opts for a life as a tree alone in the forest and anchored to the ground. The story stresses the absolute terror and irrational fear that accompanies a "refusal of the call". The image elaborated here is of a hare fleeing a hound, and the terror of feeling the hot breath of pursuit at the back of the neck. Apollo, a god of love, has been transformed into a vicious hound. This analogy illustrates how challenges can grow into monsters, if not faced. Imagine experiencing this chase in a dream and feeling the terror. Like Daphne, we would run away from the nightmare. Unable to fight, we'd have taken flight. We'd also pay a price, aside from the loss of a night's sleep. In the emotional, imaginative realm of the mind, challenges not confronted grow in intensity. Fear thrives within our mind until it becomes automatically irrational, and any link to its cause becomes something to be avoided at all costs. Such reinforcement of fear becomes the birth of a phobia.

The myth of Daphne can be seen as a flight from love and sex and all its disruptive emotions. But the inner, emotional pattern delineated by this myth is the same as the avoidance of any challenge. Think of the first time you got up in front of an audience to give a speech. Everyone knows the feeling of stage fright. If we face our fear and get over the initial nervousness, we can end up enjoying the attention. The next time it's a little easier because we understand the initial hurdle of nervousness that we must overcome. Now imagine that the first time you face an audience, your anxiety and fear become so great that, tongue-tied, you just stand there, unable to speak. The embarrassment burns deeply into your memory. The next time the opportunity arises to get up in front of an audience, you refuse. Over time the initial incident may fade from memory, but whenever you confront a similar challenge, emotional aversion springs to the fore. These emotions, often long divorced from any specific incident, grow in intensity and become irrational. Entrenched fear is a major inhibitor of action and also a barrier to creativity.

We know that fear is a major inhibitor of action and a barrier to creativity. At the extreme, fear becomes a phobia, an anxiety disorder defined by an inability to accept a challenge of adaptation. For example, a fear of heights initially prompted by some experience long forgotten, can develop into an unconscious habitual terror of heights, a phobia. The fearful response is acquired and over time reinforced until it is automatic. My wife, for example, won't drive on four-lane highways anymore. With a great deal of guilt, I remember the initiating event.

She was driving on an expressway, and it was raining hard. We got stuck behind a slow tracker trailer. I encouraged my wife to pass, but every time she sped up and got alongside the truck, she reached a point where the mist from the truck's wheels was so thick that she couldn't see anything ahead.

I yelled, "Floor it!" My wife yelled, "I can't see where I am going." We tried a number of times: I'd yell, "Pass!" and my wife would refuse because she still couldn't see where she was going. Suddenly my wife dropped back; pulled over to the side of the highway; got out of the car and walked around to the passenger side; opened the door and yelled, "You drive!"

The incident happened years ago, but ever since that day, my wife has avoided driving on four-lane highways. The discomfort of the event always springs to mind. To avoid it, she will go out of her way just to avoid an expressway. She knows the cause to be that initiating event, for which I have apologized profusely. Still, the discomfort she feels is strong enough that she avoids expressway driving.

In just this way, fear can become an impenetrable barrier. A popular fairytale describing the impact of a retreat from a challenge of adaptation is the story of Briar-Rose, one better known as Sleeping Beauty:

> Little Briar-rose (Sleeping Beauty) was put to sleep by a jealous hag .... And not only the child, but her entire world also went off to sleep. ... The king and queen ... who had just come home and were entering the hall, began to fall asleep, and with them the whole estate. All the horses slept in the stalls, the dogs in the yard, the pigeons on the roof, the flies on the wall, yes, the fire that flickered on the hearth grew still and slumbered, and the roast ceased to simmer. And the cook, who was about to pull the hair of the scullery boy because he had forgotten something, let him go and fell off to sleep. And the wind went down, and not a leaf stirred in the trees. Then around the castle, a hedge of thorns began to grow, which became taller every year, and finally shut off the whole estate. It grew up taller than the castle so that nothing more was seen, not even the weathercock on the roof. (Campbell 62-63)

The hedge of thorns grew and grew until it became an impenetrable barrier surrounding the castle. This impassable hedge parallels what happens when a painful experience from the past gives rise to anxiety. That tension gains ground in imagination, even though the specifics of the event may be forgotten. Each similar experience arouses these emotions, and the conscious mind, using habitual reaction as its guide, determines that the best response is to run, hide, and avoid the risk at all costs. The mental anxiety grows into an irrational fear and becomes an impenetrable barrier.

Embarking on the Monomythic Journey, a creative act, requires taking a step beyond the normal and comfortable world we know. To do so sets in motion a process of expanding our horizons, of accepting challenges, and of working through anxiety and fear to achieve our objective. However, actual risk-taking is not much encouraged in society despite widespread admiration for high achievers. Usually, conformity is the implicitly condoned and socially rewarded path.

> The usual person is more than content, he is even proud, to remain within the indicated bounds, and popular belief gives him every reason to fear so much as the first step into the unexplored. (Campbell 78)

To step out in front of – or even to step aside from – the crowd is to become exposed. Examine the history of anyone who has ever introduced a radical new theory into the world of science or proposed a radical cultural change to revitalize a decadent society. They are viciously attacked, verbally or worse. Conformity is the glue that holds a culture together. It is a source of seeming stability. Conformity can also become the sticky tar that prevents a culture from evolving to meet the challenges of change. Because culture is based upon 'fitting in', fear of social exile is likely to inhibit its members from freely choosing to embark upon a monomythic adventure.

However, within the mythic realm, the emotion of fear that waits at the boundaries of the unknown is symbolically represented by the Threshold Guardians:

> Such custodians bound the world in the four directions -- also up and down -- standing for the limits of the hero's present sphere, or life horizon. Beyond them is darkness, the unknown, and danger; just as beyond the parental watch is danger to the infant and beyond the protection of his society danger to the member of the tribe. ... Thus the sailors of the bold vessels of Columbus,

breaking the horizon of the medieval mind -- sailing, as they thought, into the boundless ocean of immortal being that surrounds the cosmos, like an endless mythological serpent biting its tail -- had to be cozened and urged on like children, because of their fear of the fabled leviathans, mermaids, dragon kings, and other monsters of the deep. (Campbell 77-78)

The Threshold Guardians of fear invoke caution, prevent ill-advised passage and frighten the timid.

In effect, the Threshold Guardians are protectors, reminders that fear is a warning that may be worth heeding. The Guardians serve to inspire second thoughts before a path of action is undertaken. Here is a simple dream that reflects the protective nature of the Threshold Guardians:

"I dreamed," stated a middle-aged, married gentleman, "that I wanted to get into a wonderful garden. But before it there was a watchman who would not permit me to enter. I saw that my friend, Fraulein Elsa, was within; she wanted to reach me her hand, over the gate, But the watchman prevented that, took me by the arm, and conducted me home. 'Do be sensible -- after all!' he said. 'You know you mustn't do that.'" (Campbell 82)

The contemplation of an extra-marital affair with all its potentially destructive impact on family is brought to consciousness in the depth of a dream by a Threshold Guardian in the guise of a watchman.

Threshold Guardians also prevent too easy passage into the realm of adventure. "For the realm of adventure, the realm of the mind, is a realm of unleashed emotions and an unfettered imagination. It is a realm of all possibilities." The Greek Myth of Phaethon is a story of a too-easy passage where no Threshold Guardian was encountered:

> Born of a virgin in Ethiopia and taunted by his playmates to search the question of his father, he set off across Persia and India to find the palace of the Sun --for his mother had told him that his father was Phoebus, the god who drove the solar chariot.
>
> … Climbing the steep path, Phaethon arrived beneath the roof. And he discovered Phoebus sitting on an emerald throne, surrounded by the Hours and the Seasons, and by Day, Month, Year, and Century. The bold youngster had to halt at the threshold, his mortal eyes unable to bear the light; but the father gently spoke to him across the hall. "Why have you come?" the father asked. "What do you seek, O Phaethon -- a son no father need deny?" The lad respectfully replied: "O my father (if thou grantest me the right to use that name)! Phoebus! Light of the entire world! Grant me proof, my father, by which all may know me for thy true son." The great god set his glittering crown aside and bade the boy approach. He gathered him into his arms. Then he promised, sealing the promise with a binding oath, that proof the lad desired would be granted.
>
> What Phaethon desired was his father's chariot, and the right to drive the winged horses for a day.

"Such a request," said the father, "proves my promise to have been rashly made." He put the boy a little away from him and sought to dissuade him from the demand.

"In your ignorance," said he, "you are asking for more than can be granted even to the gods. Each of the gods may do as he will, and yet none, save myself, has the power to take his place in my chariot of fire; no, not even Zeus."

Phoebus reasoned. Phaethon was adamant.

...

"If, at least, you can obey your father's warnings," the divinity advised, "spare the lash and hold tightly to the reins."

...

"But hurry! While I am speaking, dewy Night has reached her goal on the western shore. We are summoned. Behold, the dawn is glowing. Boy, may Fortune aid and conduct you better than you can guide yourself. Here, grasp the reins."

Tethy, the goddess of the sea, had dropped the bars, and the horses, with a jolt, abruptly started; cleaving with their feet the clouds; beating the air with their wings; outrunning all the winds that were rising from the same eastern quarter. Immediately -- the chariot was so light without its accustomed weight -the car began to rock about like a ship tossing without ballast on the waves. The driver, panic-stricken, forgot the reins, and knew nothing of the road.

...

The chariot, having roared for some time through unknown regions of the air, knocking against the stars, next plunged down crazily to the clouds just above the ground; and the Moon beheld, in amazement, her brother's horses running below her own. The clouds evaporated. The earth burst into flames. Mountains blazed; cities perished with their walls; nations were reduced to ashes.

...

Mother Earth, shielding her scorched brow with her hand, choking with hot smoke, lifted her great voice and called upon Jove, the father of all things, to save the world. "Look around!" she cried at him. "The heavens are asmoke from pole to pole. Great Jove, if the sea perish, and the land, and all the realms of sky, then we are back again in the chaos of the beginning! Take thought! Take thought for the safety of our universe! Save from the flames whatever yet remains!"

Jove, the Almighty Father, hastily summoned the gods to witness that unless some measure were quickly taken all was lost. Thereupon he hurried to the zenith, took a thunderbolt in his right hand, and flung it from beside his ear. The car shattered; the horses, terrified, broke loose; Phaethon, fire raging in his hair, descended

like a falling star. And the river Po received his
burning frame.

The Naiads of that land consigned his body to a
tomb, where upon this epitaph:

Here Phaethon lies: in Phoebus' car he fared,
And though he greatly failed, more greatly he
dared. (Campbell 133-136)

Note that the epitaph has a note of commendation in it: in the
mythic realm, it is always better to have tried and failed than
never to have tried at all.

In myth, the hero's physical death is seldom a result of failure,
yet failure is always possible, to show us what to avoid in
the future. The story of Phaethon can be seen as symbolic of
the dangers of over-indulgent parenthood. If too restrictive as
parents, we set the stage for a child to build a thorny hedge
of fear, restricting their horizons, while on the other hand,
being too indulgent can equally court disaster. The Threshold
Guardian role of parenthood is an art.

The Threshold Guardians of myth symbolize both caution in
facing the unknown and wide-awake awareness whenever
we undertake a challenge, where the outcome is uncertain.
The ultimate fear, of course, is the fear of death. But symbolic
death is a precursor of rebirth, and rebirth is frequently the
description given to a revelatory experience:

Everywhere, no matter what sphere of interest
(whether religious, political, or personal), the
really creative acts are represented as those
deriving from some sort of dying to the world;
(Campbell 35)

At any point in our life, we are the sum total of all the choices we have made and all the experiences and knowledge we have accumulated. All that we are lies embedded in the reservoir of knowledge and experience within our minds. The Monomythic Adventure can result in the destruction of cherished beliefs that lie at the core of who we are. A revelatory experience can mean the destruction of our world as we know it. This is the shattering of the cage of Mythlock. This is the symbolic death that precedes rebirth into a newer, broader world. A fear of death is the ultimate Threshold Guardian.

We have all encountered Threshold Guardians. Whenever we feel nervous or anxious undertaking a new challenge, we experience the emotional reality of the Threshold Guardians. If we feel fear embarking on an adventure or undertaking a task tinged with danger, we experience the emotional reality of the Threshold Guardians. Whether we are aerial skiers competing in the Olympics or we are climbing onto the roof of our house to clean out the eaves' troughs, fear must be overcome if we are to successfully proceed.

The Monomythic Adventure is a journey into the Garden of the Goddess, the purely emotional realm of the mind. Within this realm, feelings create the landscape; feelings generate the images. This is the realm of dreams that can be weird or wonderful, exciting or nightmarish. Within this realm, we experience events in the reality of human emotional response. We feel them as if they are real. Remember Pan? If we wander into his dark forest unaware, he is capable of scaring us to death. The terror of nightmares that leave us sweating and shaking is as possible as the feelings of awe and wonder and either can be encountered within the Garden of the Goddess. Fear has no place in the Adventure. Fear breeds monsters of the mind. Fear, a Threshold Guardian of mythology, must be overcome before the Adventure begins.

The Magic Amulet

... though omnipotence may seem to be endangered by the threshold passages and life awakenings, protective power is always and ever present within the sanctuary of the heart and even immanent within, or just behind, the unfamiliar features of the world. One has only to know and trust, and the ageless guardians will appear. (Campbell 72).

The barriers to creativity are ubiquitous. Mythlock is rampant because we are unaware that the meaning we perceive is a product of the myths of our minds and we are unaware that these myths of our minds hide information from us that is irrelevant to the meaning they create. Scapegoatism flourishes because, as creatures of habit, we are puppets yanked about by the strings of an instinctual response. And the Threshold Guardians of fear are everywhere. Our cultures use fear to promote conformity. One step beyond the norm and peer pressure springs to the fore. Despite these obstacles, creative genius still pops up in the world in the most unlikely places. Genius seems to appear by accident. But Our Mythic Heritage clearly shows that there is a period of incubation because heroes are not born -- heroes are made.

Some people are always curious to see what lies beyond the horizon. They crave the feelings that accompany new experiences. They get restless if they are not building something or learning something new. This is the urge that prompts people to travel and see the world or go on to university when all their friends are following other paths. Curiosity is an attribute of the hero. It entices the heroes of the world to undertake the Adventure and break new ground. Heroes are made, not born. and there are events in their past that laid the foundation for their seemingly innate curiosity. The nature of these preparatory events is documented within Our Mythic Heritage.

There are myths and folktales where the son or daughter of the ruler of the land is secretly placed with a humble woodsman and his wife to be raised as one of their own. Within Christian mythology, Moses is probably the most familiar story. Moses was born to poor Jewish parents, slaves to the Pharaohs of Egypt, but at a critical moment, he was placed in a floating basket, set to drift on a river, and discovered by a princess who raised him as one of her own. Now, the Moses story is backward to most mythological equivalents. In most stories, the child's parents are kings and queens and the child is left to be raised by poor and humble folk. The story follows the process of the child, over time, coming to know that a broader, richer, and more exciting world is their true heritage. In Moses' case, it was at least a different heritage. Jesus is, perhaps, the most famous Christian example. He was the son of god placed in the home of a humble carpenter. What are the mythmakers who created these tales trying to communicate?

We are all products of the environments we grow up in. Science has shown that the brain of a child is wired in early childhood. This is eminently logical considering that a child must adapt to the environment in which he or she finds themselves to survive. We grow up in a family and where we fit in and who we are, is defined by this milieu. The political, social, economic, and religious beliefs of our culture further shape our environments and define what is and what is possible. We inculcate all of these influences and they become the unconscious, habitual, invisible myths of our minds. They define the limits of our world. But what if we believed that we were secretly the child of some rich and famous parents? What if we believed that a richer, more exciting life was our actual heritage? This could lead us to believe that existing limitations do not apply to us. This could lead us to believe that all we need to do is claim our heritage to achieve our rightful destiny.

This is the message of these myths. This is the reality behind the idea that within every human child is limitless potential. We are not bound by the defined boundaries of our existing culture. A broader, richer, expanded horizon is a possibility for all of us. But most of us never realize this fact because our limits are always stressed and never our limitless potential. We are trapped in the cage of Mythlock and unaware of our captivity. The heroes of the world become aware of this greater potential. This is a lesson learned in a hero's childhood in preparation for the heroic events of adult life.

The psychological equivalent to these mythic tales is quite common. As a young boy, I became absolutely convinced that I was an orphan adopted by my current parents. I have no recollection of where this idea came from. I remember scouring the drawers and cedar chest in my parent's bedroom looking through all their important papers absolutely convinced that I would find adoption papers. I knew it was true and this certainty was burnt into my mind. Of course, it wasn't true, but I believed it. In time this childish notion passed but buried deep within my repertoire of knowledge and experience was and is the emotional residue of this childish belief. The experience became an unconscious myth of my mind. Whenever I felt trapped by limited options, the feelings aroused unconsciously recalled the pattern of this belief and I knew that I was not limited by the dominant values of my situation. This also led me to believe, occasionally, that I was not bound by the rules, which caused me endless trouble in school.

The dream of orphanhood is a relatively common human experience. But if you look up the interpretation that has been attached to the dream through the objective scholarly approach, you again find negative interpretations much like what occurred with the Narcissus myth. This interpretation sees the orphan dream as a symbol of rejection, abandonment, sadness, and frustration. If you empathetically feel as the mythic child felt, or as I felt as a real child having this dream, the interpretation is much more positive. This or some experience like it is a preparatory event in the lives of would-be heroes or creative geniuses. It doesn't make them heroes or geniuses, but it is auspicious. It contributes to the creation of an attitude of curiosity and a belief, even if unconscious, that a greater destiny than exists before them can be theirs.

Curiosity may be an attribute of the hero, but a hero requires many other characteristics to succeed. How do heroes overcome the fear that the Threshold Guardians instill in most of us? Where does the hero acquire the confidence and courage needed to overcome the pressures of conformity? Where does the hero acquire the perseverance and determination that success can be achieved when all the odds are against it? Science is proving that a loving, nurturing, and caring environment in a child's early years goes a long way to achieving this objective. But, again, the answer also lies in the stories of Our Mythic Heritage.

The Monomythic Adventure is a journey into a magical landscape powered by emotions and populated by the creations of unfettered imaginations. It can be frightening, as we have all experienced in nightmares. Uncontrolled emotions can generate hideous monsters. Yet heroes cross the threshold unencumbered by the fear of the Threshold Guardians. How do they do it?

In many mythological stories, the hero's or heroine's first encounter on the Adventure is with a fascinating personage. Whether it is a Spider-Woman of the American Indians or the fairy godmothers of the European folklore tradition, these characters give the hero or heroine a Magic Amulet to carry with them, which can be called upon in a moment of direst need.

> ... the first encounter of the hero-journey is with a protective figure (often a little old crone or old man) who provides the adventurer with amulets against the dragon forces he is about to pass. (Campbell 69)

The hero receives a Magic Amulet, insurance, that no matter how challenging the adventure, assistance is always close at hand. Remember Buddha's thunderbolt used as a last resort against the sticky-haired monster. The hero is warned not to waste the Magic Amulet or use it frivolously but he or she knows that it is there if needed. The image is one of reassurance that imparts the confidence that lies at the heart of the courage of a hero.

The function of the idea of the Magic Amulet was brought home to me through an experience with my daughter. She was four years old and starting school for the first time. She was about to leave the comforts of home and venture out by herself into a larger, unknown world. This was a challenging experience for my daughter as well as a trying experience for her parents. The event in question occurred in the middle of the night. I woke up to whimpering sounds coming from my daughter's bedroom. I tiptoed into her room. There was enough light from the street coming through the window and I saw my daughter murmuring and rolling around in bed. I quietly asked her what was wrong and whether I could be of any help. My daughter was asleep, but she told me a monster was after her. Now what could I do to help my daughter come to grips with the challenge of a monster in a dream? I didn't want to wake her up. The idea I came up with was the Magic Flashlight that when flashed upon a monster in the dark corner of a room would change that monster into a chair with clothes thrown over the back. Without waking my daughter, I touched her hand and said that here was a Magic Flashlight that could make monsters disappear. Shortly after my daughter settled down and I was able to get back to bed. During the entire experience, my daughter never woke up.

In the morning, I was curious about what had happened. I went downstairs and there was my daughter all nicely dressed up for her first day at school sitting at the table and eating her cereal. I asked her if the Magic Flashlight had made the monster disappear. Without a moment's hesitation, my daughter turned her head and looked at me like I was some kind of idiot. "Flashlights don't make monsters disappear," she said, "it just blinded him for a minute so I could get away!" and she returned to eating her breakfast.

I was flabbergasted. All the magic of my flashlight had been stripped away by a four-year-old and turned into a reality-based strobe light. My daughter as well as her parents survived the first day of school and many other firsts since then. Many years later I asked my daughter if she had ever used the Magic Flashlight again. She thought for a moment and said no. But she did remember other dreams where she was being pursued by monsters. These times, she said she seemed to reach a point in her dream where she'd had enough, so she just stopped and turned around to face the monster only to have the monster disappear. Now that is magic! Within the depths of her mind, my daughter learned that when you stop and face challenges, they are either cut down to size or made to entirely disappear.

Her need for a Magic Flashlight had passed. She learned that when you face a challenge it can be overcome. The essential message of the images of the Magic Amulets of mythology is, just that, a sense of confidence that any challenge faced can be overcome, especially when on an adventure in the realm of the mind.

My personal experience of a magic amulet was quite different from my daughter's. It happened when I was quite young and in a series of dreams. My experience took place over a period of three nights in three separate but similar dreams or should I say nightmares. The first night I found myself wandering through a dark maze with high, solid, impenetrable, shrub walls on all sides. Within the maze, I heard a growling sound. I wandered around trying to find my way out of the maze avoiding the source of the frightening sound that seemed to get closer no matter which way I turned. I rounded this one corner and there it was, the ugliest, large-tooth, drooling, red-eyed monster I had ever seen. I turned and ran and could hear the thrashing of the bushes of the monster in pursuit. I couldn't find a way out and suddenly I found myself trapped in a dead-end. I tried climbing the walls but the hedge, while impenetrable, was all leaves and I couldn't find a solid branch to climb. The monster was getting closer. I was trapped. The only way out was up so I started flapping my arms frantically. Wonder of wonders in this realm of all possibilities, I began to feel myself slowly rising off the ground. I increased my effort until finally, I reached the safety of a large overhanging branch. When my heart stopped pounding, I smiled. I could fly.

The next night, I am not sure that it was the very next night or a few nights later, I found myself again trapped within the maze, but I felt much more confident. The ground was familiar, and I knew there was always a way out. This time when I encountered the monster, I turned and ran until again I was caught in a dead-end. I quickly flapped my arms and flew to the safety of the overhanging branch. When the ugly monster arrived, I laughed and taunted him, and he roared in rage.

The third night I was cocky. I actually sought out the monster. When I found him, I ran and taunted him. I even let the monster get close a couple of times and laughed at his slow lumbering pursuit. His rage was deafening. I outran the monster until, sure enough, I again found myself trapped in a dead-end. The monster was still far behind so I waited and yelled that he couldn't find his own nose even if he tripped over it. Soon the monster came into sight as he rounded the corner of the dead-end isle. I let him move closer because I knew I could get away any time I wanted. Cautiously the monster approached until I thought it was time to leave. I started flapping my arms, but nothing happened. I looked down and saw that as I had waited my feet had sunk into mud over the tops of my shoes. As I tried to lift one foot the other foot only went deeper. I flapped my arms frantically, but I could not break free. The monster stopped and a smile formed on its ugly mouth and his drooling increased. I kept trying harder and harder, but nothing worked. Then at some point, I realized the futility of my effort and I stopped flapping my arms. I remember feeling disgusted with myself for my stupidity and arrogance. At the very moment I surrendered to my fate, I felt something strange. I felt myself slowly rising into the air. I looked down and saw my shoes come free from the mud, at which point I started flapping my arms as hard as I could, just barely reaching the safety of the overhanging branch as the monster leaped toward me. My cockiness was gone, and I felt an overwhelming sense of awe and wonder. Totally helpless, having exhausted all the resources at hand, and yet, at the direst moment of all some mysterious force had come to my aid. This magical force is the power of the Magic Amulet.

Within dreams, we feel as if what is transpiring is real. We feel the emotions as if the events were actually happening. We experience the events in the reality of human emotional response and within our memories these events are registered in a similar way, as if real. They too become part of our repertoire of knowledge and experience. They too become the myths of our minds creating the reality that we perceive. The lessons learned in the realm of dreams become a source of the attitudes and beliefs that we carry with us throughout our lives. A hero's confidence is the reality symbolized by the Magic Amulets of mythology.

If we examine the emotional core of these dreams we discover another parallel. The dreams start with overwhelming feelings of discomfort. In both cases, my daughter's and mine, we were under attack by monsters. Fear, verging on terror, was the feeling that dominated. Then by magic, a magic flashlight in one case and the ability to fly in the other, a solution is manifest, escape achieved, and the feelings of despair replaced by elation or at least relief. This is the same emotional pattern as the Adaptive Response. The start of the process is feelings of discomfort that arise when we encounter a situation that we do not understand or cannot handle. These feelings of discomfort are the harbingers of the Adaptive Response. We struggle to understand to escape these feelings. Then a moment's distraction, surrender, or abandonment of the struggle by the conscious mind and the miracle of inspiration occurs. It's as if our conscious struggle to find an answer has to get out of the way so our unconscious mind can reveal the path. We find a new perspective, a new way of looking at the situation that gives rise to new opportunities, and new possibilities, and with this, the emotions of discomfort are dispelled.

This is the emotional pattern, the commonality that underlies all Adaptive Responses, all revelatory experiences, all moments of inspiration, all acts of creation, and all religious or mystical experiences. It is the emotional pattern underlying all Monomythic Adventures. When we experience an event in reality, we experience it emotionally. When we experience an event within a dream, we experience it emotionally. Whether experienced in reality or the depths of a dream, the event becomes a part of our repertoire of knowledge and experience. Whenever we encounter a situation in the future with the same emotional coloring, our previous experience of the Adaptive Response is available to spring to the fore. We know the pattern; we know there is a way out; we know there is a solution. This knowledge, whether conscious or unconscious, is the Magic Amulet that can help us face any challenge. This awareness, whether conscious or unconscious, is the secret of a hero's confidence.

In the last of my flying dreams, one specific aspect of the Adaptive Response is highlighted. As a little boy in the dream, I knew I could fly, but when I found myself stuck in the mud I still escaped. A mysterious force came to my aid. I was rescued, apparently, by a power beyond myself. In mythological terms this is called 'supernatural aid' (Campbell 69). When the conscious mind gets involved in trying to make sense of this emotional phenomenon, we get a myriad of wild explanations. "I was rescued by the hand of god." "A guardian angel came to my aid." Whatever rationalization is devised to explain the phenomenon, we come to believe that help is always at hand. We come to know that no matter how difficult the situation may get we will find a way out. This knowledge of the creative process, this Magic Amulet, even if unconscious, is the secret of creative genius.

The psychological reality behind the Magic Amulet is the unconscious knowledge that no matter how helpless and lost we get; the miracle of inspiration is always at hand. If our experience of this emotional pattern behind the creative act is, in the least way familiar, in moments of need it will spring to the fore, break us out of our perceptual box and reveal information previously hidden so we can devise an understanding leading to an appropriate action or understanding. If our experience of this emotional pattern happens frequently, it can even become habitual. If habitual, the creative act occurs regularly, and we have creative genius. Creative genius is not some inherited trait bestowed upon some and denied others but merely a habit of mind and emotion. This is the secret, as we shall see, of the Masters of Two Worlds.

Knowledge and experience that tells you that the miracle of inspiration is always at hand is the Magic Amulet of the hero. Whether consciously or unconsciously and regardless of the rationalization used to explain it, this is the source of the amazing confidence that imbues great men and women who accomplish impossible feats. They know that no matter how difficult the challenge, help is always at hand. And whether their conscious understanding of the process is knowledge of the psychological reality of the inspirational process or the idea that a Guardian Angel is resting on their shoulders is immaterial. The emotional assurance of the Magic Amulet is what carries them forward.

> ... though omnipotence may seem to be endangered by the threshold passages and life awakenings, protective power is always and ever present within the sanctuary of the heart and even immanent within, or just behind, the unfamiliar features of the world. One has only to know and trust, and the ageless guardians will appear. (Campbell 72)

This Magic Amulet is the source of the power of faith, whatever rational or irrational explanation is devised by the conscious mind to provide understanding. This is the source of the confidence of the great men and women of history.

> "I feel myself," said Napoleon at the opening of the Russian campaign, "driven towards an end that I do not know. As soon as I shall have reached it, as soon as I shall become unnecessary, an atom will suffice to shatter me. Till then, not all the forces of mankind can do anything against me." (Campbell 72)

The confidence or knowledge that the magic of inspiration is ever at hand is the essence of the meaning of the Magic Amulets of mythology. Instilled with the confidence of a Magic Amulet we are ready to cross the threshold of the Magic Door and enter the Garden of the Goddess. Finally, the Monomythic Journey can begin.

Beyond the Magic Door

Rescue from Without

Within the libraries of recorded history lie the means to escape despair through a mythic 'rescue from without'.

In the mythical realm, beyond the Magic Door lies the Garden of the Goddess. But before we step into the Garden, there is one very significant aspect of the creative experience that we need to explore. It is much like the eureka phenomenon involving a gift from the Goddess, a new perspective, but seemingly avoiding a trip into the Garden. Young children naturally inhabit the Garden of the Goddess. Their minds are fluid and powered by curiosity and fearless confidence. In the early days, they explore their worlds by observing everything going on around them. They try this and that, over and over, until they figure out how something works. They are always busy building a repertoire of knowledge and experience in order to adapt, survive, and flourish in the world around them. This is learning, the most significant and lasting component of any Monomythic experience.

Learning doesn't stop when early childhood ends but it does change. No longer is it just the creation of an understanding but frequently it is the modification of an existing understanding to incorporate new information. Learning slows down when we are no longer frolicking around in the Garden like a child, but it doesn't stop. Learning only stops when we find ourselves ensconced within the cage of Mythlock.

Education continues the process of learning. Higher education is encouraged because the more we learn the better prepared we are for the challenges of life and the better the chance we have of achieving the goal of 'living happily ever after'. Learning plays a large role in the Monomythic Adventure as the mythic tales covering the experience of a 'Rescue from Without' attests.

Have you ever been reading a book when you start to really understand what the author is trying to say? Suddenly you understand and start to see the implication of the author's message. There is excitement and a feeling of accomplishment that often accompanies the moment. Mythically you have received a gift from the Goddess, a new perspective, the author's perspective and his words are enriched with more meaning. This is the joy of learning and a major avenue to successful adaptation. It happens whenever you discover a new idea in a book or somewhere else, and absorb it so that it can provide a new perspective and hence new meaning and understanding. This is the nature of a mythic 'rescue from without'; information from the external world provides the means to understand and remove the discomfort of not knowing.

I remember back in the sixties Marshall McLuhan's book, Understanding Media. It became a run-away fad during my university days. McLuhan saw all man's creations as 'extensions of man,' providing a framework, or perspective, for understanding their impact upon our world. The automobile, for example, was seen as an extension of our legs. Imagine and feel what it would be like to have legs so long that you could walk a hundred miles in an hour. You might travel a hundred miles just to visit a nightclub in the big city for a single evening. You might even travel a hundred miles just to see a ball game. Prior to this growth in our legs, a trip of a hundred miles would not have even been contemplated except as a summer excursion. This extension of man, the invention of the automobile, transformed not only our social fabric but also transformed acres of farmland into concrete expressways.

McLuhan's idea that man's inventions could be understood as extensions of man's capabilities provided a metaphor for understanding a myriad of aspects of modern culture and their impact on our lives. McLuhan saw the electronic media as an extension of our nervous systems. He saw the early stages of the convergence of computers and the telephone and predicted the Global Village long before the Internet or cell phones were words in common parlance. If we can see, talk and interact with people from the other side of the world, it is like we are living in the same village and suddenly all the implications of village life apply to the entire world. We live in this world now and most of the troubles of today can be explained as failures of adaptation of members of isolated cultures, to the reality of living in a Global Village.

When I was in public school, for example, the only strange people I met were white Anglo-Saxons who spoke a different language. I can't remember the first time I saw a black man in real life. I only saw them in movies as poor, uneducated people or criminals. At that age, I never met an indigenous person, but I saw the savages in the wild west movies. Today, walking down the street you encounter people from all races and speaking all manner of languages. No wonder we all are having so much trouble adapting to a Global Village when we have been harnessed to such disgusting systemic racism for years.

McLuhan's book helped me understand the culture I was living in by providing me with a 'rescue from without'. The fad that gripped thousands of people during that time was indicative of the effectiveness of his perspective in helping others come to an understanding of the dramatic changes taking place in their world. Looking to the external world for answers to nagging questions is the role of higher education, except in those schools that think preparing people for the job market is their primary purpose.

I was in my first year of university when I had my mind-blowing monomythic experience. It was wildly wonderful, but I had no idea what was going on. So, as a would-be scholar, I began my research and discovered Joseph Campbell. In his book, The Hero with a Thousand Faces, I found thousands of descriptions of what was happening to me. I learned that our mythic heritage was filled with mythic descriptions of these inner emotional/mental events. I also learned that by empathizing with the mythic characters I could emotionally experience the event they were describing. I learned to feel as they felt in order to learn as they had learned. Campbell's ideas became a 'rescue from without' for me. These were the most exciting years of my life.

I had noticed that religious imagery frequently poked its head into the explanations of revelatory experiences. In the early days of my research, I had the idea that if the Adaptive Response lay at the heart of every hero's adventure, it could provide a peek into the minds of real-world heroes. In the West the initiator of the dominant religion, Christianity, met all the criteria of a hero, so I researched the life and times of Jesus of Nazareth.

In the first pages of my research into his life, I immediately ran into mythic imagery in the story of Jesus. Jesus thought he was an orphan. His father was god and he was placed in the home of a humble carpenter and his wife, to be raised. Here was the myth that planted the idea within the mind of a child that they were not limited by the boundaries of their current environment. Its purpose is to give the child the confidence that great things can be accomplished. Well, in Jesus's case, great things were accomplished.

It also didn't take long to confirm for me, that the Adaptive Response is actually at the heart of Jesus' message. He did not have access to the mythic tales of the past to explain his experience because there were no public libraries those days in Nazareth. Jesus was forced to describe his experience in his own words. For example, the impact of the fluidity of the mind within an Adaptive Response experience, where I used the words:

> To him or her that it is given
> Much more shall he or she receive.

is referenced in Matthew 13:12.

> for whoever has, to him more shall be given, and
> he
> will have an abundance.

The idea that the myths of our minds create the meaning we perceive, where I used the words:

> We become what we behold, and
> We behold what we've become.

is referenced in Luke 11:34-36

> Your eye is the lamp of your body. When your eyes are good, your whole body also is full of light. But when they are bad, your body also is full of darkness. See to it, then, that the light within you is not darkness. Therefore, if your whole body is full of light, and no part of it dark, it will be completely lighted.

This is a description of an escape from the blindness of Mythlock. Again and again, in the story of Jesus, I discovered parallels to the mythic tales from Joseph Campbell's Monomythic Adventure. His act of baptism is a classic symbol of rebirth, an escape from Mythlock, and the opening of our eyes to a new world. Jesus' message is the message of the Monomythic Adventure. I was so excited about my discovery that I wrote a book: The greatest hero: the genius behind the myth. It is not dry research material but a retelling of his story in poetry. Essentially, I rewrote the bible, at least the New Testament portion.

The adaptive response lies at the heart of all religions and all religious experiences. This common emotional/mental pattern of experience is the source of all the wildly different rationalized constructs devised by the conscious mind to explain a revelatory experience. All religions stem from this natural, innate emotional mental adaptive response of their founders. Troubled by a challenge of adaptation affecting his or her life or the lives of his or her tribe, a hero undertakes a Monomythic adventure. With the new light of inspiration cast upon the problem, the hero's conscious mind devises a new adaptive strategy. He or she returns to share this strategy with their fellow man and a new religion is born.

If you experience a crisis that brings on depression and despair, mythically you have entered the belly of the whale. You can find escape through a 'rescue from without'. The story of Jonah's descent into the belly of the whale and his subsequent rescue by god is one of the most famous cases. The story of Little Red Riding Hood is another. She is caught by the wolf and devoured. Locked in the belly of the wolf, she is rescued by a hunter who kills the wolf, slits open his belly, and pulls Little Red Riding Hood free. This is a mythological 'rescue from without', rescue from a crisis by absorbing and using some idea already existing within the world.

In a crisis, rather than looking inward towards the Goddess, we most often scan the outer world in search of help. Many answers, to the challenges we face, exist in the world, particularly in the world of philosophy and religion. Personal escape from the belly of the whale is achieved when we absorb one of these ideas, put it on like sunglasses, and see the world effused with the new meaning it creates. The absorption of these new perspectives can produce a dramatic experience that can change our lives. This is the liberation from depression that can lead a person to shave their head, put on a long robe, pick up a tambourine, and with an inner glow of contentment begin to solicit funds in an airport concourse. This is the liberation from despair that can lead a person to run off with some obscure cult to forge a new life in the wilderness. Thankfully, most often, this is the liberation that rescues us from despair and lets us live a normal happy life. This is an escape from the belly of the whale brought about by a 'rescue from without'.

The great philosophies and religions of the world arise from the Monomythic Adventures of their founding fathers. The stories of their lives are the stories of their struggle to make their ideas a common understanding. Religions exist in every corner of the world. Religions are ubiquitous because they serve a critical purpose. They provide a comprehensive adaptive strategy for their adherents. They provide understanding and guidance for living from the cradle to the grave and for some of them even beyond. They can give life purpose and meaning. They create community. For their adherents, religion provides certainty amidst confusion, order out of chaos, stability in turmoil, a lifeline in crisis, and the warm comfort of a like-thinking community.

But there is a price that must be paid for the comforts and inspirations of any group-wide adaptive strategy. The cohesion that holds together the members of a group or religion requires agreement on the basic principles upon which the group is founded. A like belief system is the core. In the early years of most religions, there are always struggles against heresies. Over the years religions clarify and solidify the tenets of their beliefs. This is a common evolution of religion. Slowly over time they solidify, codify, and firmly establish a set of beliefs. This is the hallmark of stability --- commonly held beliefs and habitual or even ritual responses to life's daily challenges. While this clarification of beliefs increases the cohesion of the group it also decreases the flexibility of the adaptive strategy. Religions develop orthodoxy. The result is Mythlock. And as a religion becomes mythlocked so do its hundreds, thousands or even millions of members become mythlocked. This is cultural Mythlock. This is not a problem if the culture continues in a world without significant change. But change, some say, is the only constant, and in our current era, rapid change is the most dominant reality.

A 'rescue from without' may resolve the problem and remove the discomfort, but it happens without a step across the threshold of the Magic Door. A Monomythic Adventure is an escape from Mythlock. The Garden of the Goddess is a fluid realm with unfettered emotions. The adventurer who enters the Garden re-experiences the fluidity of mind he or she lived as a child. On our adventure in the Garden, if hampered by ingrained biases, we may encounter the Hag or the Seductrice. But beyond these challenges lies an encounter with the Goddess in all her splendor and the emotions of that moment are beyond ecstasy. At this point in the adventure, you may even experience an ascend up the Stairway to the Stars and learn the power of more comprehensive perspectives to free you forever from the trap of Mythlock. This is what awaits the adventurer within the Garden of the Goddess.

The Garden of the Goddess

Within the Garden of the Goddess, the realm of
the mind, lies all the human heart could ever
desire.

As we have seen, the barriers to inspiration are many. The
stability of culture is based upon conformity and this conformity
is cultural Mythlock, an inhibitor of creativity. Scapegoatism
tricks us into believing that the source of our problem and the
solution lies beyond ourselves and the Threshold Guardians of
fear make us timid. The way around these barriers lies along
the path of the hero.

Most documented adventures of the heroes of mythology are
initiated by emotionally troubling challenges of adaptation.
Something changes or something goes wrong and there
appears no simple answer to the problem. A once reasonably
happy life is shattered, and we don't know what to do about
it. This is a challenge of adaptation beyond the scope of the
hero's existing knowledge and experience. The first step of the
adventure is introspection, a step across the threshold of the
Magic Door into the Garden of the Goddess.

The Garden is the mythical equivalent of the realm of the human
mind. It is a realm of all possibilities. It is a realm of unfettered
emotions and an unfettered imagination. It is a plastic, fluid,
realm where the landscape and time are malleable. But it is also
a world bound by the horizons of our existing knowledge and
experience. The hero enters the garden still blinded by Mythlock.
The challenge is to break out of the current perceptual box into
a broader world where the answer we seek lies.

The nature of the Garden of the Goddess that one enters on a Monomythic Adventure is not foreign to our experience. We experienced it as a child of course, and as an adult, we also have knowledge of the nature of this realm because we dream. The dream world is the mythic Garden of the Goddess. This is where the Goddess dwells. It is here that she dispenses her boons of inspiration. It is here that we may experience a Meeting with the Goddess. It is possible to enter this realm when fully awake. Wild flights of fantasy leading to exciting inspirations are equivalent waking experiences. In the nineteen sixties, some people experimented with the drug LSD, lysergic acid diethylamide. The drug removes inhibition and induces an emotional state of mind equivalent to an emotional visit to the Garden of the Goddess. These experimenters soon learned that the result could be good trips or bad trips. The bad trips could be very traumatic, shattering the stability of the mind. These experimenters of the sixties learned the necessity of creating an atmosphere of calm serenity to set the stage because they learned that the realm of the mind is a realm of emotion and that errant negative emotions could lead to a bad experience. In the dream world, in the realm of the mind, in the Garden of the Goddess, negative emotions breed monsters of the mind. Forgive me if I repeat myself but this is a critical piece of awareness.

The world of dreams and the Garden are similar and dreams themselves are equivalent to mythic stories in both their nature and their purpose. We saw how a magic flashlight and a maze with a monster, both experiences within dreams, provided emotional experiences to the dreamers. Myths can be viewed as merely externalized dreams.

> Dream is the personalized myth, myth the depersonalized dream; both myth and dream are symbolic in the same general way of the dynamics of the psyche. (Campbell 19)

Every night we sleep, and we dream, so the psychologists and our Fitbits say. Every night we venture into this wondrous realm of the mind where anything is possible. Sometimes we may even wake up remembering our dreams. We may even awake with a boon. Have you ever woken up in the morning with the solution to a problem that has been nagging you? Whether we remember our dreams or not we do wake up in the morning usually refreshed and ready to face another day. Sleeping and dreaming are critical human functions.

> Without our regular, minor night journeys in sleep, we would soon become victims of mental desiccation. Dreaming is ... the equivalent of artistic experience, [often our] only means of self-transcendence, of breaking away from the trivial plane and creating [our] own mythology. (Koestler 360)

Nightly we sleep and nightly we dream. Nightly we undertake a journey into the Garden of the Goddess.

The Garden is a realm of all possibilities, and the Goddess encompasses all. While she can be manifest in the joy and excitement of discovery, she is equally capable of manifestations of horror. An encounter with the horrible aspect of the Goddess is a bad trip. Bad emotional experiences in the Garden cannot only shatter mental complacency; they can also shatter mental stability. Stories from our mythic heritage warn us of the dangers.

> One quiet afternoon Ramakrishna beheld a beautiful woman ascend from the Ganges and approach the grove in which he was meditating. He perceived that she was about to give birth to a child. In a moment the babe was born, and she gently nursed it. Presently, however, she assumed

a horrible aspect, took the infant in her now ugly
jaws and crushed it, chewed it. Swallowing it,
she returned again to the Ganges, where she
disappeared. (Campbell 115)

Imagine the wild swing of emotions that you would go through
if you witnessed this event. Imagine observing the miracle of
birth and the wonder and awe of a mother suckling a beautiful
newborn child. Then, suddenly a dark shadow of a thought
passes through the mind and all the images of wonder are
transformed in a flash of an eye into images of abject horror as
the woman, now a monster, devours her offspring. This is an
image of an encounter with the Horror of the Goddess. This
is an image of a bad trip. This is an image of how negative
emotions in the Garden of the Goddess can breed monsters of
the mind.

The psychological reality of a mythic encounter with the Horror
of the Goddess is traumatic. The pattern of experience is a
sudden wild swing of emotion from an exciting, glorious high of
one moment, to the deepest, darkest pit of hell in the next. I was
reading a poem by a late eighteenth-century poet one evening
when the poem triggered a wonderful flight of fancy. I have
since tried to find this poem but without success, which leads
me to believe that while a poem may have triggered the idea,
the contents of the fantasy were entirely of my own imagining.
The idea triggered by the poem was that this poet, long before
man had even gotten off the ground, envisioned a world where
airplanes spanned the globe. These planes introduced people
from different cultures and allowed the sharing of ideas. These
planes made possible the sharing of goods between continents
so that even locked in the depths of winter, fresh vegetables
and fruits were always available. The idea grew into an image
of paradise and a worldwide Utopia and I marveled that the

mind of a man from that time period could envision a world of airplanes long before they ever existed.

I was flying high on adrenaline during this Utopian excursion when suddenly it dawned upon me that I lived in the era where airplanes spanned the globe, and it was hardly Utopia. Suddenly a shadow flashed through my mind and I saw hundreds of dark silhouettes flying through the sky and out of their bellies they disgorged tons of explosives killing thousands of men, women, and children in the cities below. One moment I was flying high riding a glorious vision and the next I was plunged into abject horror. Physically it felt like I had just dropped flat on the souls of my feet from ten feet in the air. An electrical shock raced through my body. I shook like a leaf and my heart was pounding. The event was imaginary, transpiring within my mind, but I experienced it in the reality of human emotional response. It felt real. I went for a long, long walk that night waiting for the shaking to subside and my heart to stop pounding. Mythically, I had experienced an encounter with the Horror of the Goddess.

Remember, in the Garden, emotions rule. The images of dreams and myths are symbolic of feelings. In dreams, the problem, challenge, or crisis we face is manifest in images based upon the intensity of our discomfort and derived from our own personal fears. Small challenges produce small images of fear. Major challenges breed monsters of the mind. I experienced this emotional swing from elation to horror while I was wide awake. More familiar to most of us is the horror of the nightmare. We can wake up from a nightmare with our hearts pounding and sweat pouring down our faces just like it was a real event. On the other hand, feelings of wonder and awe can breed visions of beauty beyond imagination. Reality is composed of both. Within the Garden of the Goddess:

> The devotee is expected to contemplate the two with equal equanimity. Through this exercise his spirit is purged of its infantile, inappropriate sentimentalities and resentments, and his mind opened to the inscrutable presence which exists, not primarily as "good" and "bad" with respect to his childlike human convenience, his weal and woe, but as the law and image of the nature of being. (Campbell 114)

In the Garden of the Goddess, we float on a cushion of emotion where feelings of the moment transform the landscape. This is the realm of 'supernatural wonder.' This is the Garden of the Goddess, the creative realm of the human mind.

The architecture of the world's great cathedrals is designed to instill a proper emotional state, upon entry. These edifices with their sky-high arches and magnificent columns instill awe and wonder in those who enter. Entering from the noisy street and crossing the threshold is symbolic of passing from the 'world of common day' into the 'world of supernatural wonder.' These visual images instill feelings of respect that have us whispering so as not to disturb the silence of the cathedral.

> ... the approaches and entrances to temples are flanked and defended by colossal gargoyles: lions, devil-slayers with draw swords, resentful dwarfs, winded bulls. These are the threshold guardians to ward away all incapable of encountering the higher silences within. They are preliminary embodiments of the dangerous aspect of the presence, corresponding to the mythological ogres that bound the conventional world, or to the two rows of teeth of the whale. They illustrate the fact that the devotee at the

moment of entry into the temple undergoes a metamorphosis. His secular character remains without; he sheds it, as a snake its slough. Once inside he may be said to have died to time and returned to the World Womb, the World Navel, the Earthly Paradise. The mere fact that anyone can physically walk past the temple guardians does not invalidate their significance; for if the intruder is incapable of encompassing the sanctuary, then he has effectually remained without. Anyone unable to understand a god sees it as a devil and is thus defended from the approach. Allegorically, then, the passage into a temple and the hero-dive through the jaws of the whale are identical adventures, both denoting, in picture language, the life-centering, life-renewing act. (Campbell 92)

A step across the threshold into the Garden of the Goddess, the World Womb, the World Navel, the Earthly Paradise, or Heaven itself is an imaginative step into the realm of the human mind.

Within the Garden, the Adventure begins. It is emotional because it is the emotions that blaze the new synaptic paths to new ways of looking at things so we can discover answers to our questions or new ideas to revitalize our lives. But first, we must be prepared for the Adventure because as the Horror of the Goddess attests, this can be a dangerous place. Our emotions must be groomed in front of the Looking Glass as soon as we enter the Garden. The Looking Glass itself can be an impenetrable barrier because out of the Looking Glass can arise the images of hell and why religious mythology says that the gates of Paradise are barred to evil men and women.

The Looking Glass

We are the authors of our lives because it is not the events of life that make us who we are but our responses to those events.

During the creative act, after we have broken out and discovered a new perspective, our conscious minds draw upon the contents of our existing knowledge and experience, and any other information available, to devise a reasonable understanding. The validity of any devised understanding is determined by our feelings. If it is beautiful, it makes us feel good and is accepted. If it doesn't, it is rejected, and the conscious mind devises another meaning. In subsequent chapters, we will examine mythic images that explore this interaction between our conscious minds and our feelings in more detail, but the motivation of the conscious mind during the creative act is to devise meaning that makes us feel good or at least dissipates our discomfort.

This same motivation in everyday life leads the conscious mind to set aside those memories that reflect badly on us as well as purposely suppressing traumatic events so we can get on with our lives. If unsuccessful in suppressing the emotions of a traumatic event, we have a psychological problem. There is no percentage for our conscious mind, with a motivation to make us feel good, to dwell upon memories of past experiences or traumas that only make us feel bad. These events tend to be glossed over, forgotten, or suppressed. This is why nostalgia always has such a nice glow about it. Only the good times are remembered. Our conscious mind creates a rosy image not only of things past but also of ourselves. Uncomfortable feelings tend to be suppressed. Here in lies the rub for the Monomythic adventurer. The Garden of the Goddess is a realm of unfettered emotions. No bulwark of rationalization or forgetfulness can prevent the liberation of suppressed feelings within the Garden of the Goddess. Dealing with the liberated feelings of guilt, regret or anger is the essence of the trial of the Looking Glass and the first challenge we may face after we step across the threshold of the Magic Door.

A moment's honest introspection will reveal that most of us have feelings of guilt about some event, no matter how minor. Somewhere, sometime, we have all made mistakes that have caused others pain. Similarly, most of us have some regrets. We may regret actions not taken, love not returned, or some choices made. Feelings of guilt and regret are common. Still, others may harbor anger for some abuse or trauma inflicted upon them. This anger can be bottled up inside. Even with these feelings of guilt, regret, or anger buried in our unconscious, they still infect our everyday attitudes. But once we step across the threshold into the Garden of the Goddess, these suppressed emotions are unleashed because the Garden of the Goddess is a realm of unfettered emotions.

Within the Garden inhibitions are set aside and suppressed emotions unleashed. This is a necessity of the creative process. Any restraints upon feelings must be removed to achieve the fluidity of mind required for the creative process. But this is a realm where errant negative emotions breed monsters of the mind. Before we can safely navigate this fluid realm our emotions must be groomed in front of the Looking Glass. Here, we confront the unleashed feelings of guilt, regret, or anger often long suppressed. In front of the Looking Glass, we must find forgiveness for our transgressions. In front of the Looking Glass, we must also find forgiveness for those who have transgressed against us, which is how we remove the yoke of anger from around our own necks. In the mythology of the Monomythic Journey, our emotions are groomed in front of the Looking Glass so we can safely navigate the emotionally fluid realm of the mind. In the mythology of religion, standing in front of the looking Glass is called Judgment Day.

The experience of the Looking Glass is that moment when our lives flash before our eyes. Stripped of all illusions we get to relive, in the reality of human emotional response, those events in our lives that shaped us into the person we've become. Like Narcissus seeing himself reflected in a 'pool of shiny silvery water,' we come to know ourselves. In front of the Looking Glass, we are forced to face the unleashed emotions of guilt, regret, or anger.

> In the vocabulary of the mystics, this is the second stage of the Way, that of the "purification of the self," when the senses are "cleansed and humbled," and the energies and interests "concentrate upon transcendental things"; or in a vocabulary of more modern turn: this is the process of dissolving, transcending, or transmuting the infantile images of our personal past. (Campbell 101)

It is possible to flash across the threshold without encountering the Looking Glass if all that is sought is a simple answer to a simple problem. But if the precipitating event is an emotionally charged crisis in our lives, we will encounter the trials of the Looking Glass.

Mythology has plenty of images symbolizing the trials of the Looking Glass. There are the rocks that crush, the reeds that cut, and the fires that burn, but at the center of the experience is seeing yourself stripped of all illusion like this description taken from a modern fantasy novel, The Sword of Shannara.

Early in the story, it is predicted that the hero, a young boy, will gain possession of the sword of Shannara with which he will destroy an evil wizard. The sword of Shannara is a magic sword. Once grasped by our young hero it initiates a Looking Glass experience.

> Thrust suddenly before his eyes, the world that was his birthplace and life source, from past to present, lay open and revealed to him, stripped bare of his carefully nurtured illusions, and he saw the reality of existence in all its starkness. No soft dreams colored its view of life, no wishful fantasies clothed the harshness of its self-shaped choices, no self-conceived visions of hope softened the rawness of its judgments. (Brooks 690- 692)

Once our young hero touches the sword he is thrust in front of the Looking Glass. It is here that he comes to know himself. It is here he confronts his liberated feelings of guilt, regret, or anger.

> Here was an accounting of every hurt he had caused to others, every petty jealousy he had felt, his deep-seated prejudices, his deliberate half-truths, his self-pity, his fears -- all that was dark and hidden within himself. (Brooks 690- 692)

Feelings of guilt, regret, or anger, candy-coated, forgotten, or suppressed, are liberated and must be confronted. This is the emotional reality of a Looking Glass experience.

The 1990 Joel Schumacher film, Flatliners, written by Peter Filardi is unique in that it is an entire movie dedicated to exploring the nature of the Looking Glass experience. The story is about a group of medical students who decide to explore life after death by killing themselves and being revived after a short period of time. This is the flatline experience. The experiments take place in a museum with the outer walls covered with gargoyles, symbolic of the fact that all who pass must leave fear behind. Although part of the experience transpires while they are supposedly brain-dead, most take place within their minds after they have been revived. The filmmaker uses a red glow and other cinematic devices to symbolize the fact that these are events transpiring within their minds. The characters that participate in the experiment undergo a Monomythic Adventure and although the movie concentrates upon the Looking Glass experience, the characters pass through the trials of the Looking Glass and receive a gift from the Goddess. They gain a new perspective and are liberated from the burden of guilt that they have been carrying with them throughout their lives.

Dave Labraccio is the atheist, skeptic character in the movie. He is also a very caring person as shown by his willingness to sacrifice his career as a doctor to do what he believes is right -- although not yet a full doctor he performs emergency surgery that saves a woman's life, and he gets suspended as a result. His caring is also shown when he volunteers to undergo the flatline experience in the hope of preventing Rachel, his love interest, from taking part in the dangerous experiment. His Monomythic experience starts with the classic life flashing before his eyes. The experience of seeing himself starts with a collage of images from the last few days, regressing through childhood until he encounters an image of himself within his mother's womb. Next, he finds himself flying over snow-covered mountains, above the clouds, scanning a wonderful panoramic view of the world, until he hears the sounds of children playing; sees the flash of a subway train entering a dark tunnel and the face of a little girl staring at him. After he is revived, the journey continues. When actually on the subway, he hears his name called. He turns and the same little girl starts walking toward him calling him names and taunting him. She has a wonderful string of negative epithets and soon all the subway passengers are laughing at him, and his embarrassment reaches a point of discomfort verging on tears before he suddenly flashes back to reality. Later we see him standing outside the fence of an empty schoolyard, remembering it filled with playing children and he sees himself with others teasing and taunting the same tearful little girl. He tracks down the whereabouts of the little girl, who is now twenty-six and takes a two-hour drive to her house to apologize. He apologizes for being a jerk so long ago. The scene ends with her accepting his apology and Dave finds forgiveness and passes through the Looking Glass.

Rachel, Dave Labraccio's love interest, is a beautiful, young, driven doctor with an obsessive interest in death. She believes there is a better place after death, but she seems to need reassurance. Her Monomythic experience starts with the image of Christ, her magic amulet, in a picture hanging on the wall. As a child, she re-experiences her soldier father's homecoming party and feels the joy of his return. Then she finds herself irresistibly drawn towards a bathroom door where she has been told never to go when her father is inside. She enters and sees only her father's back just before her mother comes and yells at her. Her father, realizing that his daughter is there, rushes out of the room, almost trips on her tambourine, slips down the stairs, rushes outside, and a loud gunshot echoes through the scene. Her mother rushes outside and Rachel follows and sees a large bullet hole surrounded by blood in the windshield of their truck. Her father has killed himself and the young Rachel sees herself as the cause. After she is revived, her journey also continues. She starts to see the face of her father everywhere, in mirrors, and even a corpse during bisection class. Asked how she feels she says, "Fine for someone who keeps seeing her father who's been dead for twenty years." Later, in her mind, she finds herself back again in her old house on that fateful day.

She sees her mother ironing and is again irresistibly drawn toward the forbidden door. This time, as an adult, she enters the room, and looking over the shoulder of her father she sees him injecting drugs into his arm. Her father turns, sees her, and asks her forgiveness. The scene ends with them hugging each other and she says, "It's alright Daddy." as she passes through the Looking Glass having confronted a misconception of guilt created as a child.

The main character in the movie is Nelson. He is the one who came up with the idea for the experiment. He says the experiment is "quite simply to find out if there is anything out there beyond death. Philosophy has failed; religion has failed and now it's up to the physical sciences." His journey begins with him, two friends and his dog running across a field of flowers. Then he sees his dog barking at something up a tree and the first experience ends with him facing a young boy in a subterranean walkway. Nelson's trip is far from over. After he is revived, he marvels at his heightened senses as he hears sounds from the street he's never heard before. Sitting alone, he hears a dog and realizes that it is his dog, Champ. He notices that his dog is severely injured. That night he dreams, but this time he sees himself, two friends, and his dog chasing a little boy across a field of flowers until he experiences himself falling face-first out of a tree and awakes hyperventilating.

Nelson becomes seriously paranoid and is stalked within his mind by the little boy who inflicts punishment on him every time they meet. In his dreams, he relives the incident where the little boy is up a tree and he is throwing rocks at him from below. In time we find out that, as a kid, Nelson was responsible for the death of a boy named Billy Mahoney, and at nine years old Nelson was sent to a reform school as punishment. His dog, Champ, was injured by a falling branch during the incident. Although killing Billy Mahoney was never intended, it was the result of Nelson's actions. The suppressed feelings of guilt for causing the death of another human being are liberated during Nelson's flatline experience and must be confronted.

To escape his paranoia, Nelson decides he must undergo the flatliner experiment again. Before he does he calls Rachel, who has just made it through her Looking Glass experience and when she says, "It doesn't matter." he answers," Everything matters. Everything we do matters." This time the images that Nelson experiences are changed. This time he is the boy being chased; he is the boy up the tree; he is the one hit by the rock; he is the one who falls to his death under the tree. The filmmaker, using the real-world electric shock to revive him, has Nelson wake up beneath the tree with Billy Mahoney standing over him. Billy removes his hood and smiles at Nelson who then says, "Thank you." Nelson is revived and with the forgiveness of Billy Mahoney, he too passes through the Looking Glass.

Suppressed emotions of anger are not explored in the movie. This is the anger of the victim towards the perpetrator of some abuse or horror in their lives. The horror of the event may have been suppressed and forgotten to allow one to carry on with life, but in the Monomythic realm, these feelings are liberated during the Looking Glass experience and must be confronted. In hospitals where older people are feeling the closeness of death, many experience the trauma of released emotions stemming from childhood abuse or other traumatic events in their lives. Herein lies the real tragedy of the victims of abuse or violence. Imagine seeing yourself reflected in the Looking Glass and reliving your life up to the instance of trauma. It was a good life and could have been a wonderful life, but instead, it becomes warped and twisted by anger and the urge for revenge stemming from an incident of horror or abuse. This is the real tragedy of the victims of abuse and violence, lives warped and twisted by anger or fear. Horrific emotional events not dealt with and transcended can warp a person's life. The Looking Glass experience brings out in stark relief, the meaning of the words, 'forgive us our trespasses,' but equally stark are the words, 'forgive those who trespass against us' for only through forgiveness can we free ourselves from the yoke of anger around our own necks. One implication of this insight is astounding. The quality of our lives is not determined by the events of our lives but by our responses to those events.

In the movie examples of the Looking Glass experience, the feelings released were the feelings of guilt or even misconceptions of guilt. Rachel faced a childish misconception of guilt associated with her father's death. Nelson had to confront the guilt associated with causing the death of another human being, which stemmed from an accident precipitated by a senseless childish act. Nelson experienced the event, the source of his guilt, from the perspective of Billy Mahoney. It was Nelson himself up the tree; it was Nelson himself hit by the rock; it was Nelson himself falling to his death from the tree. This is the nature of the Looking Glass encounters with feelings of guilt. We get to experience the pain of those we have transgressed. Now, imagine for a moment being someone responsible for the brutal murder of another human being. Imagine experiencing, in the reality of human emotional response, the terror, torment, pain, and torture of your victim. Here in lies the source of all the images of hell.

The fantasy novel, The Sword of Shannara, is about a mythical sword. This sword once touched initiates a Looking Glass experience. The young hero's task in the novel is to use the magic sword to vanquish an all-powerful evil wizard. Our young hero has no skills relevant to the handling of a sword, yet he is supposed to destroy the evil wizard. Prophecy has predicted his victory but when the wizard is finally confronted, our hapless hero is quickly disarmed. Defeat seems imminent.

All hope is gone. But the touch of the magic sword initiates a Looking Glass experience. Suddenly the evil wizard is thrust in front of the Looking Glass and confronted with all his evil deeds, and he experiences the pain and torment of his victims. The evil wizard is destroyed by this confrontation. In Christian and Muslim mythology, the Looking Glass experience is Judgement Day. This is the moment when evil deeds are confronted, and, if necessary, the fires of hell ignited.

On highly emotional Monomythic Adventures, frequently, the first event across the threshold is this moment of ultimate introspection. Our lives flash before our eyes and we re-experience, in the reality of human emotional response, those events that molded us into the persons we've become. Reflected in the Looking Glass, we come to know ourselves. Many Monomythic Adventures start and end with the Looking Glass experience because this experience itself imparts to the adventurer many adaptive advantages. By finding forgiveness for the guilt and regrets one has accumulated in one's life, those burdens are removed from our shoulders. By forgiving those who trespass against us, we remove the yoke of anger from around our own necks. This is liberating. The crisis that initiated the adventure can even be rendered inconsequential by the Looking Glass experience. But liberation from the burdens of guilt, regret, or anger is the least significant potential adaptive advantage to be gained through the Looking Glass experience.

The Looking Glass experience is the ultimate experience in self-awareness. We come to truly know ourselves. We come to understand how we act and react, appropriately or inappropriately to the events of our lives. We come to understand how we perceive and misperceive. We catch a glimpse of some of the faulty myths residing within our repertoire of knowledge and experience. We get to see the good and bad within ourselves. These less-than-exemplary bad habits often cause problems in our lives without our awareness. If it is a good life that we are after, these bad habits once recognized must be dealt with. This is the meaning behind these lines from Christian mythology.

> If your right eye causes you to sin, gouge it out and throw it away. It is better for you to lose one part of your body than for your whole body to be thrown into hell. (Matt 5:29-30)

An adaptive lesson learned through the Looking Glass experience is that if you are having troubles in your life look first within yourself for habits that cause people to react negatively towards you and when you find them, eliminate them, and your life will improve.

Self-awareness has even more adaptive advantages. If we know ourselves, we can better understand the world of man. We are human beings and through understanding ourselves we gain insight into the actions and reactions of other human beings. We can observe the tragedy of domestic abuse and see its source in the same emotional pattern we follow when shouting at our wives or girlfriends after we have foolishly locked the keys in the car. We can observe the reactionary backlash of governments in power against change and see its source in our own reaction to new and foreign ideas. 'Know thyself' becomes the secret to understanding the world of man and the more accurately we understand this world the better our chance for successful adaption.

The experience of the Looking Glass has still more lessons to impart. As our life flashes before our eyes, we learn that we are the sum total of all the experiences, choices, and decisions that we have made in our lives. By inference, we learn that we are the authors of the persons we've become. We are not some helpless twig pushed along by the tide of events. We are in charge because it is not the events of life that make us who we are but our responses to those events. We are in control because we control our responses and with this understanding, there is an end to helplessness. We are the authors of our lives and although we may not be able to control the world around us, we are in control of our responses to that world. We are the masters of our own ships. We create ourselves and we can re-create ourselves. With this understanding comes liberation, strength, and power. Here is one source of strength common to all heroes. They know that they are in control of their lives, and it is in their power to accomplish what it is they wish to accomplish.

If the Looking Glass experience is not the terminating event of the Adventure, there are new challenges to face. Emotionally we may be groomed for the adventure, but the initiating problem or crisis yet remains. The adaptive challenge remains unresolved. But even within the Garden we remain trapped by Mythlock, blinded by the myths of our minds. Until we debunk the myth, which is hiding the information we need to devise a more appropriate adaptive response, the treasure we seek remains hidden. Even within the Garden, we behold what we've become, which is why the Goddess has many manifestations. A negative response to the strange can precipitate an encounter with the Goddess as Hag. A negative attitude towards our sensual natures may transform the Goddess into the Seductrice. If we escape these impediments and receive a gift from the Goddess, a new way of looking at things, we can experience the joy of inspiration. But the Goddess always promises more. Should we meet with the Goddess in all her splendor and glory, we can be changed forever. We can be reborn. But even as wonderful as the experience of rebirth may be, the Goddess still promises more. Beyond the Goddess lies the Stairway to the Stars, the ultimate experience awaiting any Monomythic Adventurer.

The Hag

The mind likes a strange idea as little as the body likes a strange protein and resists it with similar energy. (Koestler 216)

The Goddess is a mythic image of our heart's desires. Most of our mythology is the creation of men so the images of our heart's desires are embodied in the female. But the feelings underlying the images apply equally to women.

> Woman, in the picture language of mythology, represents the totality of what can be known. The hero is the one who comes to know. As he progresses in the slow initiation which is life, the form of the goddess undergoes for him a series of transfigurations: she can never be greater than himself, though she can always promise more than he is yet capable of comprehending. She lures, she guides, she bids him burst his fetters. And if he can match her import, the two, the knower and the known, will be released from every limitation. (Campbell 116)

> And when the adventurer, in this context, is not a youth but a maid, she is the one who, by her qualities, her beauty, or her yearning, is fit to become the consort of an immortal. Then the heavenly husband descends to her and conducts her to his bed. ... And if she has shunned him, the scales fall from her eyes; if she sought him, her desire finds its peace. (Campbell 119)

Within the Garden of the Goddess lies all the human heart could ever desire.

All we need to live wonderful happy lives lies within the Garden, the realm of our minds. Through the creative act, we devise an understanding that provides a strategy we can use to create wonderful, exciting, successful, happy lives. If we are happy with our lives, all's well. If not, a Monomythic Journey can help. The Adventure is the quest for understanding whether an answer to a simple problem or a resolution to a crisis or just the desire to improve the quality of our lives. The Looking Glass experience grooms our emotions for the Adventure. But while our emotions may be calmed by the Looking Glass experience, all that we perceive upon entry into the Garden remains conditioned by our emotions and the existing myths of our minds. Within the Garden, we remain, if less securely, in the grip of Mythlock. We behold what we've become. This is the psychological reality that gives rise to the many manifestations of the Goddess.

The gift of the Goddess is always a new way of looking at things, a new perspective. The new perspective reveals information previously hidden. The conscious mind uses this newly revealed information to devise a new understanding. But the creative act is an emotional event. An intellectual understanding, a product of our conscious minds alone, is not enough. Until a new idea is emotionally embraced it remains an intellectual concept. Not until absorbed emotionally does it become a new myth of our minds creating meaning to the raw data of our senses. Not until the new idea becomes a myth in our minds are the implications and full potential of the idea revealed.

When presented with a new idea, at first, we do not fully understand it. Not understanding anything causes some discomfort. Therefore, as human beings we tend, initially at least, to react negatively to new ideas because new ideas can be disturbing. The avoidance of discomfort is the motivation of our conscious minds. Success is achieved, from the perspective of our conscious minds, when discomfort is dispelled or at least kept at bay. So, our initial response to a new idea is to reject it. Our conscious mind scurries about looking for holes, inconsistencies, or weaknesses in the new idea in order to build a rational reason for rejection. And our conscious mind is assisted in this rejection by the existing myths of our minds, which can be tenacious in their self-preservation. They filter out any information irrelevant to the meaning they create and can completely hide the significance of any new idea. This is Mythlock, the trap of habit, and habits are hard to break.

Since within the fluid realm of the mind, where our feelings generate the images we encounter, our natural negative response to the new can transform the image of the Goddess herself.

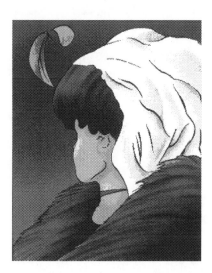

In the picture above, do you see a Hag or the Goddess? The Hag seems to dominate, reflecting the reality of our initial response to the strange and unfamiliar. It can be difficult to absorb a new idea when our conscious mind rejects it to protect us from discomfort and the invisible myths of our mind filter out potentially supporting information. Because of our natural, human, negative response to strange and foreign ideas, the Goddess is frequently encountered in the guise of the Hag.

The image of the Hag for women can have many other negative connotations besides a symbolic manifestation of the initial feelings of rejection and disgust when confronted by a new idea. The image of the Hag is the creation of a male-dominated mythic heritage. But whether male or female the natural human response to new and foreign ideas is identical. There is a fairy tale expressing this idea without any reference to the image of the Hag. This is the Grimm fairy tale of "The Frog Prince."

> "Long long ago, when wishing still could lead to something, there lived a king whose daughters all were beautiful, but the youngest was so beautiful that the sun itself, who had seen so many things, simply marveled every time it shone on her face. Now close to the castle of this king was a great dark forest, and in the forest under an old lime tree a spring, and when the day was very hot, the king's child would go out into the wood and sit on the edge of the cool spring. And to pass the time she would take a golden ball, toss it up and catch it; this was her favorite plaything.

> "Now it so happened one day that the golden ball of the princess did not fall into the little hand lifted into the air, but passed it, bounced on the ground, and rolled directly into the water. The princess followed it with her eyes, but the ball disappeared, and the spring was deep, so deep

that the bottom could not be seen. Thereupon she began to cry, and her crying became louder and louder, and she was unable to find consolation. And while she was lamenting in this way, she heard someone call to her: 'What is the matter, Princess? You are crying so hard a stone would be forced to pity you.' She looked around to see where the voice had come from, and there she beheld a frog, holding its fat, ugly head out of the water. 'Oh, it's you, old Water Plopper,' she said. 'I am crying over my golden ball, which has fallen into the spring.' 'Be calm; don't cry,' answered the frog. 'I can surely be of assistance. But what will you give me if I fetch your toy for you?' 'Whatever you would like to have, dear frog,' she said; 'my clothes, my pearls, and jewels, even the golden crown that I wear.' The frog replied, 'Your clothes, your pearls and jewels, and your golden crown, I do not want; but if you will care for me and let me be your companion and playmate, let me sit beside you at your little table, eat from your little golden plate, drink from your little cup, sleep in your little bed: if you will promise me that, I will go straight down and fetch your golden ball.' 'All right,' she said. 'I promise you anything you want, if you will only bring me back the ball.' But she thought: 'How that simple frog chatters! There he sits in the water with his own kind and could never be the companion of a human being.'

"As soon as the frog had obtained her promise, he ducked his head and sank, and after a little while came swimming up again; he had the ball in his mouth and tossed it on the grass. The princess was elated when she saw her pretty toy. She picked it up and scampered away. 'Wait, wait,' called the frog, 'take me along; I can't run like you.' But what good did it do, though he croaked after her as loudly as he could? She paid not the slightest heed, but hurried home, and soon had completely forgotten the poor frog -- who must have hopped back again into his spring." (Campbell 49-50)

The king's daughter ..., the day following the adventure at the well, heard a thumping at her castle door: the frog had arrived to press her to her bargain. And in spite of her great disgust, he followed her to her chair at the table, shared the meal from her little golden plate and cup, even insisted on going to sleep with her in her little silken bed. In a tantrum she plucked him from the floor and flung him at the wall. When he fell, he was no frog but a king's son with kind and beautiful eyes. And then we hear that they were married and were driven in a beautiful coach back to the young man's waiting kingdom, where the two became a king and queen. (Campbell 119-120)

If we explore the emotional core of the pattern in this story, it starts when the ball is lost. A problem arises that causes discomfort and unhappiness. Then a solution to the problem manifests itself but because of our natural, negative, emotional response to a new or foreign idea, it appears in the guise of an ugly frog. The idea is rejected; the princess runs home. But new ideas can be persistent once revealed; the frog follows the princess home. The princess is disgusted and repulsed but then something happens. In a fit of anger, she throws the frog against the wall and instantly regrets her hasty action. Suddenly her perspective changes, she looks sympathetically at the frog. She acquires a new way of looking at the idea and it is transformed. The ugly frog becomes a prince. A new way of looking at things is absorbed and a new world with new potential is revealed to the princess. This story delineates the emotional pattern inherent in the initial negative response to a new idea and the potential positive impact after its absorption. Here is the delineation of the entire hero myth, the creative process, in the story of a little girl and a frog that turns into a prince.

There is an Irish myth that delineates this same emotional mental pattern of behavior symbolically presented as an encounter with the Goddess as Hag. In this story, five brothers encounter the Goddess in her ugly guise. In four cases, although the answer to their quest, symbolically expressed as water to quench their thirst, lies right before their eyes, they are repulsed, revolted, and disgusted by what they see. In the fifth case, Niall, not only accepts what he sees but embraces the idea and his world is transformed.

> A story ... is told of the five sons of the Irish king Eochaid: of how, having gone one-day ahunting, they found themselves astray, shut in on every hand. Thirsty, they set off, one by one, to look for water. Fergus was the first: "and he lights on a well, over which he finds an old woman standing sentry. The fashion of the hag is this: blacker than coal every joint and segment of her was, from crown to ground; comparable to a wild horse's tail the grey wiry mass of her hair pierced her scalp's upper surface; with her sickle of greenish looking tusk that was her head, and curled till it touched her ear, she could lop

the verdant branch of an oak in full bearing; blackened and smoke-bleared eye she had; nose awry, wide-nostrilled; a wrinkled and freckled belly, variously unwholesome; warped crooked shins, garnished with massive ankles and a pair of capacious shovels; knotty knees she had and livid nails. The beldame's whole description in fact was disgusting. 'That's the way it is, is it?' said the lad, and 'that's the very way,' she answered. 'Is it guarding the well thou art?' he asked, and she said: 'it is.' 'Dost thou license me to take away some water?' 'I do,' she consented, 'yet only so that I have of thee one kiss on my cheek.' 'Not so,' he said. 'Then water shall not be conceded by me.' 'My word I give,' he went on, 'that sooner than give thee a kiss I would perish of thirst!' Then the young man departed to the place where his brethren were, and told them that he had not gotten water."

Olioll, Brian, Fiachra, likewise, went on the quest and equally attained to the identical well. Each solicited the old thing for water, but denied her the kiss.

Finally it was Niall who went, and he came to the very well. '"Let me have some water, woman!' he cried. 'I will give it,' said she, 'and bestow on me a kiss.' He answered: 'forby giving thee a kiss, I will even hug thee!' Then he bends to embrace her and gives her a kiss. Which operation ended, and when he looked at her, in the whole world was not a young woman of gait more graceful, in universal semblance fairer than she: to be likened to the last-fallen snow lying in trenches

every portion of her was, from crown to sole;
plump and queenly forearms, fingers long and
taper, straight legs of a lovely hue she had; two
sandals of white bronze betwixt her smooth and
soft white feet and the earth; about her was an
ample mantle of the choicest fleece pure crimson,
and in the garment a brooch of white silver; she
had lustrous teeth of pearl, great regal eyes,
mouth red as the rowanberry. 'Here, woman,
is a galaxy of charms,' said the young man.
(Campbell 116-117)

When we get by the catalog of the ugly and the beautiful as
defined in the author's era, the story is simple. Fergus, Olioll,
Brian, and Fiachra encountered the Goddess dominated by
feelings of revulsion and disgust and they perceive an ugly
Hag. Their feelings of revulsion and disgust locked the Goddess
into her ugly manifestation.

By deficient eyes she is reduced to inferior states;
by the evil eye of ignorance she is spellbound to
banality and ugliness. (Campbell 116)

The qualities of our perceptions arise from our feelings, our
emotions, and the meaning we perceive from the myths of our
minds.

When Fergus first encounters the Goddess in her ugly
manifestation he asks, 'That's the way it is, is it?' and the
Hag answers, 'that's the very way.' Fergus accepts what is as
what always must be. He believes that all he sees is fixed and
unchangeable. He is unaware that all meaning is a product
of the myths of his mind and that a new perspective can
potentially transform all he sees. Although a resolution to his

discomfort, the water to quench his thirst, lies right before his eyes he rejects it totally and his quest is a failure.

Niall, on the other hand, didn't just consent to kiss the Hag, he embraces her wholeheartedly and she transforms into an image of the Goddess in all her splendor. This is the 'eureka moment' when what was once confusion becomes crystal clear in all its beauty and simplicity. A gift from the Goddess is a new way of looking at things. But the new meaning is not created until we embrace the new perspective, put it on like sunglasses, and let the new perspective create a new meaning to the contents of our experience and the world around us.

Fergus rejected the Goddess in her ugly manifestation entirely. He hardly stopped a moment to contemplate that the answer to his quest lay within his grasp. But even if he knew that here in lay the answer, until that idea is embraced, put on like sunglasses, nothing changes. This is a frequent point of failure in the Monomythic Adventure. Although the answer sought is found, if not embraced nothing changes. Notice there are 'five sons', a not-so-subtle reference to our five senses. The information of our five senses is rendered inadequate to the challenge by the blinding myths of our minds.

I have a friend, a classic example of an angry young man. He suffered a divorce arising largely out of his anger and became determined to figure out what was wrong with him. One evening, during a discussion, he laid out, what I saw as a complete understanding of his problem. I yelled "Eureka" and got very excited that his quest had finally born fruit. But his trial wasn't over. While he had an intellectual understanding and knew the meaning of what he was saying, he never emotionally embraced the idea, put it on like sunglasses, and let it create new meaning and a new understanding of his world. The significance of what he was saying remained hidden because he had not absorbed it emotionally and allowed it to create a new understanding of the contents of his experience.

Arthur Koestler, in his book The Act of Creation, calls this intellectual understanding of a problem without absorbing its significance, 'snowblindness.' He presents some classic examples taken from the field of astronomy, which in its early days was firmly locked into Aristotle's theories about the movement of the planets. Aristotle believed that all the planets and other heavenly bodies moved in perfect circles at uniform velocities. This belief was firmly ensconced in the minds of all the early astronomers. It initially blinded them to other, more accurate, alternatives.

> Copernicus was an orthodox believer in the physic of Aristotle and stubbornly clung to the dogma that all heavenly bodies must move in perfect circles at uniform velocities. In the fourth chapter of the Third Book of the Revolutions of the Heavenly Spheres, the original manuscript of the book contains the following lines:
>
> It should be noticed, by the way, that if the two circles have different diameters, other conditions remaining unchanged, then the resulting movement will not be a straight line but ... what mathematicians call an ellipse. (Koestler 216-217)

This is a description of the elliptical orbit of the planets that was not known at the time. Ironically, this passage was crossed out in the manuscript and never appeared in the printed version. It was left to Kepler, years later, to make the discovery of the elliptical orbits of the planets.

Kepler also had problems with 'snowblindness.'

Kepler, too, nearly threw away the elliptic orbits; for almost three years he held the solution in his hands -- without seeing it. His conscious mind refused to accept the 'cartload of dung' which the underground had cast up. When the battle was over, he confessed: 'Why should I mince words? The truth of Nature, which I had rejected and chased away, returned by stealth through the backdoor, disguising itself to be accepted. Ah, what a foolish bird I have been!"

Poor Kepler, he was even more foolish than he thought: he actually discovered universal gravity -- then rejected it. In the Preface to the New Astronomy he explains that the tides are due to the attraction of the moon, and describes the working of gravity -- even that the attracting force is proportionate to mass; but in the text of that book, and all subsequent works, he has -- incredible as it sounds -- completely forgotten all about it. (Koestler 217)

Because Kepler had not fully embraced the new idea that he stated, he did not see its dramatic implications. It was left to Newton years later, as the story goes, to see the significance of an apple falling on his head to discover universal gravity. Newton, not only embrace the idea, but he devoured it. Belief in Aristotle's theory of circular orbits and uniform velocities was so strong that this myth of the mind effectively filtered out the significance of contrary ideas for years in some of the most inventive minds of history. While this happens in science from time to time, it is rampant in our everyday world.

I am going to repeat a story, a part of which I have already told you, but add some more detail. The detail reveals how much I was impacted by the experience and how it changed my life.

I remember one summer when the four families on my wife's side got together and shared a small cottage for a two-week holiday. It was one of the rainiest summers I can remember and, of course, we were often confined to the cottage for extended periods. The five younger kids running around in such a confined space made them seem like a hundred. We all caught cabin fever and things got tense at times. Of course, when it stopped raining, all of us guys took off to play golf.

One evening returning home from a day of golf, I noticed that dark clouds were moving in over the cottage area again. Unbeknownst to me this was an omen. Perhaps the final straw for the women was the fact that we had dragged one of the older kids, although still underage, into a pub and fed him some beer. After the women had put the children to bed, including one slightly inebriated teenager, they decided that we needed a lesson in feminism. After a great day of golf and a few beers over which to exaggerate our prowess, we returned, in high spirits, to the cottage and unwittingly walked into a buzz saw.

We were under attack, and we defended ourselves. "We never helped with the dishes!" they said. This was blatantly false because each of us could remember, at least once, having put away a few dishes. "The women had to prepare all the meals!" Again, they exaggerated because we did all the barbecuing when it wasn't raining. "We always left them to look after the kids!" Well, granted that we did take off occasionally to play golf, but we had played games with the kids and when the weather allowed, we had even taken the kids on a couple of boat rides. When someone said that men didn't respect women, we knew they had gone too far. Not only did we respect women;

we loved women! One brother-in-law who had already received some feminist education tried to mediate the heated dispute. But to the women, he was a man and to us, he was a traitor to the cause. The trickster gods had a field day. We were talking through each other. While the contents of the discussion were common, the meaning perceived by each group was radically different. The women were talking faces while we were talking about a vase while both groups thought they were talking about objective reality.

Here is where I repeat the part of the story, I have already told you. One point expressed, in support of men's lack of respect for women, was men's behavior at conferences. When a man was speaking, women listened, but when a woman was talking men started aside conversations among themselves. I attend a lot of conferences and I said that was not true, because I had never seen it happen. About one month after the holiday, I was at a conference and a man was making a rather pathetic presentation when I happened to look around. Everyone was listening politely. Then a woman took the podium, and her presentation was both interesting and insightful. I believe the contrast in the quality of the two presentations helped me see the situation more clearly. I looked around while the woman was talking, and I could hardly believe what I was seeing. Four separate groups of men were quietly huddled together carrying on their own private conversations. What my sister-in-law had said was true and I was dumbfounded. As mentioned previously, at that point, I started an aside conversation myself to point out this disgusting behavior. I felt a flip like you feel when you switch from faces to a vase or a stairway to a cornice or an ugly Hag to a Goddess and a whole new world opened in front of my eyes.

I started to see a world I had never seen before. I saw intelligent women act meek, submissive, and differential towards men who were idiots. I saw slights and put-downs of women by men that were rude and at times even vicious. I saw things, although probably there all the time, that I had never noticed before. I observed discussions involving men and women and saw men dominate, ignore, and belittle the ideas of women if the women were even lucky enough to get a word in edgewise. I could not believe what I was seeing and worse, I remember doing exactly the same things myself.

Back in the office a few days later, there was a discussion about a rape trial where the man had been exonerated. The story was that this man had taken this woman out to dinner. The woman had gotten herself all dolled up and wore a sleek, seductive outfit for the evening. After dinner, he drove her home and she invited him into her apartment for coffee. Once inside he proceeded to rape her, or they had consensual sex as the man maintained. A woman in our office said that it served her right for wearing sexy clothes and inviting the man in for drinks. She asked for it! I asked this woman that if I took her out to dinner, gave her a ride home and she invited me into her house for coffee did that mean that I had a right to rape her? She said emphatically no, but I said she was wrong because that is exactly what the court had ruled. The court said that if I take you out to dinner, give you a ride home and you invite me into your house I now have the legal right to rape you. I asked her for a dinner date. She said emphatically no.

We live in turbulent times and the mistreatment of women built into our paternalistic cultures is one area being exposed to the light. The MeToo movement is revealing the depth and breadth of sexual abuse and rape within our cultures by helping those abused to overcome their trauma and publicize their experiences. A world where rich and powerful men have carried on sexual abuse and rape and covered it up with payments to silence the abused is under attack and now even losing their cases in the courts. In Canada, our amateur hockey association had a slush fund to buy silence from girls abused by young hockey players. The payments were to protect young and promising hockey players from any retribution caused by "boys just being boys". My eyes were opened by my experience at that conference years ago and the current stories in the newspapers confirm the rightness of my decision at that time to declare myself a "feminist."

The Goddess is frequently encountered as the Hag because it is a natural human reaction, for both men and women alike, when confronted with any new idea, particularly those contrary to firmly held beliefs, to react negatively. We immediately start arguing against the idea and listening only for holes or inconsistencies that can be exploited.

> 'The mind,' wrote Wilfred Trotter, 'likes a strange idea as little as the body likes a strange protein and resists it with similar energy. It would not perhaps be too fanciful to say that a new idea is the most quickly acting antigen known to science. If we watch ourselves honestly, we shall often find that we have begun to argue against a new idea even before it has been completely stated.' (Koestler 216)

This is such a common response that it is reflected in all kinds of human endeavors. In science, for example, a scientist comes up with a new theory and almost immediately he or she is vehemently attacked by colleagues who remain firmly committed or locked into the paradigm of the established theory. I can still see my brothers-in-law and me arguing vehemently against all that the women were saying long before they ever had a chance to express the ideas behind feminism. The myths of our minds effectively filtered out any information contrary to the meaning they created and hid from us the reality of the situation. In the images of mythology, our response transformed the Goddess into an ugly Hag.

New ideas initially cause feelings of discomfort. We always feel discomfort when there is something we do not fully understand. To avoid this discomfort our conscious minds, reject the idea and the existing myths of our minds assist by hiding from our conscious minds any significance inherent in the new idea. The cultures of the world are in chaos. Change is required and new ideas are being offered by those who have undertaken the Monomythic Journey and discovered possible solutions to some of the problems. One example is the problem of the homeless and those families with two jobs or more who still don't have enough to feed their families. Food banks are a solution to avoid starvation, but they don't solve the problem. The idea of sharing the enormous wealth generated by a nation, currently funding inequity, through a guaranteed annual income for the poor is an idea that can solve the problem and a few pilot projects have proven it does work. In some cases, people were able to go back to school and improve their prospects and in others the extra money they made from their jobs allowed their kids to join in the expensive sports that their wealthier friends were playing. But a common refrain from those who see the Goddess as a Hag is "I don't want my tax money going to those lazy bums," and governments in response canceled the pilot projects and the problem remains unresolved. Of course, those who are currently receiving more than their share of the nation's enormous wealth use their extra cash to buy those political candidates who agree with the 'common refrain'.

One aspect of the Monomythic Journey is the discovery of new ideas. When we react negatively to an idea, we see only its weaknesses, and its strengths are hidden. Even if we intellectually acknowledge a new idea, if we fail to embrace it emotionally, its full significance remains hidden. When we react negatively to the Goddess her beauty remains hidden and all we see is an ugly Hag. The images generated within the Garden of the Goddess are based upon our dominant emotion, and for this reason, the Goddess has many manifestations.

The Seductrice

The quality of the myths of our minds determines
the quality of our life because, maladaptations
breed sorrow and unhappiness.

All the meaning we perceive is a product of the myths of our
minds Learning is how we create these myths. Children learn
from everything around them. Research has shown that the
development of the human brain in the first few years of life
is rapid, extensive, and highly vulnerable to environmental
influences. And these influences are long-lasting (Carnegie
Task Force on Meeting the Needs of Young Children, Starting
Points, 1994). Most of the perceptual filters used to interact
with our world are created when we are children. Most of the
basic attitudes towards life are fixed when we are children.
Ironically this means that most of the meaning we perceive
results from the unconscious mythic creations of a child.

A child learns from their parents. This learning is hardly ever
the result of listening to what their parents tell them. Children
acquire their attitudes and values not from philosophical
discussion or being shouted at but from observation. Parents
are role models and children learn their basic attitudes and
values from their parents. Children are talented mimics. But
we inhabit a larger world than just the confines of a family unit.
Children also learn from their peers and how to survive within
the company of their peers. We also live in a culture, a web of
ideas based on language, economics, political philosophies, and
religious values. Every child born and raised in a particular
culture absorbs these cultural paradigms. Culture defines

appropriate and inappropriate behavior within the group. Culture is essentially group adaptation.

There are many diverse cultures around the world. Wherever there is enough isolation, cultures evolved their unique idiosyncrasies to adapt to their own unique environments. But there are areas of human adaptation that are common across all cultures. This stems from the fact that we are all members of the human species. We are all human animals with the same basic needs and desires.

One area of human nature that is most troublesome for culture is the area of procreation. Any successful culture must devise a proper strategy for the birthing and rearing of children. While reproduction is essential for the perpetuation of our specie, uncontrolled reproduction can be a disaster. This is where children end up having children and dangerous diseases can be contracted. To make matters worse our hormones start their sexual instigation while, from a cultural perspective, we are far too young to understand the consequences. To prevent the unprepared from crossing the sexual threshold too soon our culture, and religions, in particular, take on the role of Threshold Guardians. They use fear and intimidation to control the expression of human sexuality.

One strategy of the Threshold Guardians of religion and culture to rationalize their control over the manifestation of sexuality is to denigrate the sensual nature of the human animal. The idea is promoted that human beings are above nature. Our bodies, as containers of our senses and the source of feelings and passion, are relegated to the murky depths. In its place, the value of the human being is postulated to lie in the nebulous entity of the pure, pure soul.

"So long as a man has any regard for this corpse-like body," writes the Hindu monk Shankaracharya, "he is impure, and suffers from his enemies as well as from birth, disease and death; but when he thinks of himself as pure, as the essence of the Good, and the Immovable, he becomes free. ... Throw far away this limitation of a body which is inert and filthy by nature. Think of it no longer. For a thing that has been vomited (as you should vomit forth your body) can excite only disgust when it is recalled again to mind." (Campbell 123)

The perspective fostered by this attitude is a clean, orderly, sterile life. But life is not clean, orderly, or sterile. To live is to feel and the Goddess as the embodiment of the promise of a rich and rewarding life stands in stark opposition to this attitude. In the cold, sterile glare of this perspective, the Goddess is a Seductrice.

It is the nature of a healthy human animal to be curious. We see this in children. Their curiosity knows no limits until their fingers are burnt by experience or the Threshold Guardians of fear enforce conformity. But because natural curiosity is inherent in a healthy human being, it is integral to the very nature of the Goddess. It is the nature of the Goddess to encourage us to burst our fetters. It is the nature of the Goddess to always promise more and to urge us to achieve our full potential. The Goddess "lures, she guides, she bids [us] burst our fetters" (Campbell 116) in order to expand the horizon of our minds. This is the nature of the Goddess. This is the promise of the Goddess. But blinded by the veil of Mythlock and having absorbed a negative attitude towards our sensual natures, this role of the Goddess is radically transformed.

The Goddess entices us to expand our minds, expand our horizons beyond existing limitations, and explore and seek out new experiences. This is the excitement inherent in the Star Trek mantra, 'to go where no one has gone before'. This is the promise of the Goddess. If we dare, we can accomplish great things. But the meaning of all images encountered within the Garden is always a product of our minds. Feelings of revulsion and disgust, inculcated as a child, towards our sensual natures, within the realm of the mind, can transform the images of the Garden.

> Where this ... revulsion remains to beset the soul,
> there the world, the body, and woman above all,
> become the symbols no longer of victory but of
> defeat. A monastic-puritanical, world-negating
> ethical system then radically and immediately
> transfigures all the images of myth. No longer
> can the hero rest in innocence with the goddess
> of the flesh; for she is become the queen of sin.
> (Campbell 123)

With this attitude, the images of the Garden are transformed. Harvest fruits and gastronomic delights are no longer the symbols of nature's bounty but instead, become the symbols of gluttony and debauchery. The gold and silver artifacts of the garden are no longer the symbols of man's artistic nature but become symbols of man's lust for wealth and power. All the images of the Garden are transformed from symbols of nature's promise to man's excesses. From this perspective, the Goddess no longer promises to guide us beyond our limitations towards fulfillment but instead, she becomes the temptress leading us into sin and depravity. The Goddess becomes the Seductrice.

Healthy adaptation requires adaptation to reality and not a warped illusion of reality. In a mind where the Goddess has become Seductrice not only is the sense of adventure stifled but vast areas of human experience are turned upside down often in such subtle ways that we lose the connection. There was one thing that I could never figure out as a young boy. I could never understand some of my friends. All young boys like sex, want sex, and think about sex, in fact, are almost dominated by the idea of sex. So, what happens if these young boys meet a girl and have sex? The boy talks about the girl to their friends. They call her easy, a slut, a whore. They debase and degrade her in the eyes of everyone including themselves. This, to me as a young man, was an inexplicable insanity. I should state that as a young man, I was totally naive about sex and girls, while still familiar with the instinctual drive towards those goals. The innate sensual nature of young men drives them towards sex but after the wondrous feelings subside their inculcated cultural and religious values, which designate sex as filthy and disgusting, rise to the fore. The sense of guilt for having violated unconscious, inculcated religious or cultural values prompts the conscious mind to distance itself from this discomfort by reinterpreting the event as the fault of some depraved temptress leading them astray.

> The crux of the curious difficulty lies in the fact that our conscious views of what life ought to be, seldom correspond to what life is. Generally, we refuse to admit within ourselves, or within our friends, the fullness of that pushing, self-protective, malodorous, carnivorous, lecherous fever which is the very nature of the organic cell. Rather, we tend to perfume, whitewash, and reinterpret; meanwhile imagining that all the flies in the ointment, all the hairs in the soup, are the faults of some unpleasant someone else. (Campbell 121-2)

Within minds warped by a negative perspective towards our sensual natures, the girl who allows sex is no longer just a girl, but she becomes a Seductrice leading the innocent and pure, pure souls of men and boys into sin and depravity.

Negative attitudes towards our sensual natures implanted into the minds of eight-year-olds can create all sorts of warped perspectives around sex. Once an attitude is learned and deemed proper by cultural approbation, the fact that it is a learned attitude disappears from consciousness and it becomes an apparent reality. This invisible myth of mind, imparting a negative perspective on our sensual natures, can create all sorts of maladaptations. These maladaptations cause troubles in relationships between men and women and can produce horrific manifestations.

Over time and in some cultures this attitude may have diminished but it is not gone. The Threshold Guardians of our culture and religions continue to paint the area of sex as a mysterious, dark, foreboding realm of sin and depravity. Dire consequences are still promised to those who violate the cultural precepts around sex. Our immortal souls can be jeopardized. But while these more extreme attitudes towards our sensual natures may not dominate all modern cultures today, in small and subtle ways we have all been inculcated with this negative attitude. Hidden within our unconscious, habitual perceptual filters, a version of this attitude still colors our world and is reflected in attitudes and behaviors everywhere. The topic of sex is not discussed in polite company, and it is hidden from the eyes of children. This is the attitude that gets a young child's hand slapped for playing with their genitals. This is the attitude at the zoo that results in a young child's eyes being covered when animals engage in public copulation. This is the attitude that gives rise to snickering and giggling when sensuality or simple affection is publicly expressed. This is the attitude that kept, during my time, and still tries to keep, any education about sex out of the schools. Within the realm of the mind, this attitude promoted by the Threshold Guardians of culture and religion becomes embedded within our repertoire of hidden, habitual myths of the mind. It lies there lurking, ready to spring to the fore and create meaning in any sensually suggestive situation. And when it does spring forth, we react like automatons to the meaning it creates.

Girls are also inculcated with the values of their cultural and religious heritage, which denigrates their sensual natures. Of course, those girls who watch another girl who has sex suffer abuse and degradation, soon learn that it is not safe to like sex too much. They learn to adapt, to inhibit their natural sensual natures. Even within the sanctity of marriage, this inhibition can remain, and often for good reason. If a husband is inculcated with the unconscious value that says that girls who like sex are sluts and whores, and his wife exhibits an uninhibited sexual nature, the husband can come to see her as an untrustworthy slut or whore. But as if what we do psychologically within our culture was not bad enough, teaching young girls that they cannot safely like sex, some cultures do physically. Some cultures physically mutilate young girls, and remove their clitoris, so that it is physically impossible for them to enjoy the pleasure of sex. That will stop them from enticing young boys into sin and depravity!

Wherever the image of the Goddess is not that of the Goddess leading us to break free from our limitation but instead seen as that of the temptress leading us into sin and depravity, whole aspects of cultural activity are twisted. In some cultures, women are forced to cover their faces and whole bodies behind black veils. This is proscribed so innocent men will not be tempted into depravity by their own inherent sensual natures. I remember listening to the news about a country in civil war.

Women caught were raped and left lying in the road. When these girls returned to their homes and families, they were shunned and cast out as damaged goods. I heard of a story where a young girl was raped by her uncle and then murdered by her brother because she had become a blight on the family's honor.

On 16 September 2022, the Guidance Patrol, the religious morality police of the Iranian government, arrested a young, 22-year-old woman name, Mahswa Amini, because too much of her hair was showing. Apparently, the Islamic law in Iran says women and girls must cover their entire bodies so that men will not be enticed into improper behavior. As a result, the young woman died for her violation of the laws of Islam.

I have done some research into the foundations of the Christian and Islamic religions. The wives of Muhammad, the founder of Islam, were dynamic, intelligent women and active in the culture of their time. They never did, nor did Muhammad ever order, women, to hide their bodies underneath a burqa. Yet in some countries like Iran, rather than teaching young men to treat women honorably and to learn to control their own sexual urges, they demand that woman cover their bodies. Mahswa Amini's death started a revolution in the country of Iran. Wherever the image of the Goddess is transformed into the Seductrice, the whole world is upside down, and women as the external manifestation of these internal images, suffer.

Horrendous maladaptations stem from the transformation of the Goddess into the Seductrice. The need for some men to dominate and exercise control over the women in their lives is derived from this perversion. Women, as external manifestations of the Seductrice, are seen as a threat to a man's pure, pure soul. Women must be controlled to prevent them from leading men into sin and depravity. This is the attitude that declares the victim of rape the author of their own abuse. This is the attitude that leads to the horrendous abuse suffered by prostitutes. A whole range of abuse suffered by women stems from this unconscious, habitual myth of the mind, this denigration of our sensual natures, this perversion of the image of the Goddess. This is the source of misogyny.

We are all, men and women alike, as much as we act habitually, puppets on the strings of the invisible myths of our minds. Whenever we encounter a situation where the emotions of the moment call to the fore certain unconscious, habitual perceptual filters that create the meaning we perceive and upon which our actions are based, we are automatons. We all inhabit a cage of Mythlock of our own construction. If these invisible myths lead to an open healthy adaptation to life, all is well. If they lead to maladaptations, they breed sorrow and unhappiness. Only when these faulty invisible myths are made conscious can we truly break free. This is why debunking or breaking free of a myth of your mind is a critical initial step of the creative process. We may have our emotions groomed in front of the Looking Glass, but success cannot be achieved until we break free from the faulty myths that are inhibiting the discovery of a successful and joyful adaptation to our world. The struggle is worth the effort. For within the Garden of the Goddess lies all the human heart could ever desire.

Meeting with the Goddess

To him or her that it is given
Much more shall he or she receive.

A Meeting with the Goddess, in a non-perverted form (Hag or Seductrice), is the climax of the Monomythic Adventure. This is the payoff moment of the creative act. Mythologically, you receive a gift from the Goddess. Psychologically, you receive a new perspective. You see your problem in a new light and new information is revealed. With the new information, your conscious mind devises an understanding that hopefully resolves the problem, and you shout, "Eureka". Everything is beautiful, your distress is dispelled, and the feeling is wonderful. This is the boon of a Meeting with the Goddess.

The goal of the Journey is a new understanding to deal with an adaptive challenge. The goal of the moment for the adventurer is to deal with the emotional discomfort. The emotional discomfort initiating the adventure sets the tone.

> The boon bestowed on the worshipper is ... scaled to his statue and to the nature of his dominate desire: the boon is simply a symbol of the life energy stepped down to the requirements of a certain specific case. The irony, of course, lies in the fact that, whereas the hero who has won the favor of the god(dess) may beg for the boon of perfect illumination, what he generally seeks are longer years to live, weapons with which to slay his neighbor, or the health of his child. (Campbell 189)

The devised answer is usually perceived as beautiful because of the relief it provides. What generally happens on a Monomythic Journey, eager to escape the discomfort, we grasp and hold tenaciously to this first answer. We accept a boon scaled to our immediate desire. Success is achieved and the visit to the Garden ends.

If the emotions of the moment are intense, our minds become intensely fluid, and the trip may not be over. The inspirational experience can be transported to a new level.

> Experiences of this kind, when something previously turbid becomes suddenly transparent and permeated by light, are always accompanied by the sudden expansion and subsequent catharsis of the self-transcending emotions. (Koestler 328)

We can pass beyond a simple answer to our problem, to a self-transcending experience. Whenever in the presence of the Goddess, when we have 'won the favor of the Goddess,' our minds are fluid and ripe for wonders beyond imagining. It is this much more dramatic, cathartic, and self-transcending experience that embodies the full emotional meaning behind the image of a Meeting with the Goddess in all her splendor.

During my experience, I raced through all the Scapegoats until my brain got tired of finding solutions that were only rejected and decided the problem was me. Suddenly I found myself in front of the Looking Glass and realized I was the source of my own problem. It was my repertoire of knowledge and experience that was the problem, and I got a tour through my early years when it was built. My existing understanding of how the world worked was deficient. This was the source of my problem, and the gift of the Goddess was a new perspective.

The beauty of the moment was wild, and my mind was fluid and I became curious about what was happening to me. I realized later that this moment of curiosity was the ticket to an even more exciting ride. The emotions of the moment transported me beyond the requirements of my immediate need. They lead me to an experience of rebirth. In a rebirth experience, our repertoire of knowledge and experience becomes radically revised. We are radically changed. We become a child again and our minds open to the new like the mind of a child. Everywhere I looked I saw new meaning and new understanding.

The gift of the Goddess is a new perspective. The gift of the Goddess in all her splendor is multiple perspectives that create and recreate a new world around us all the time. In one instance a new perspective gives rise to a brilliant insight. A moment later another perspective on another problem produces another brilliant understanding. Also, occasionally, new perspectives can lead to the conscious mind's creation of the stupidest ideas imaginable. Thankfully, while in a fluid mental state, this reality is easily recognized and unleashes enormous laughter. This experience also leads to a critical understanding. Truth is an illusion. All we ever know is merely our mind's best guess going with the information at hand. With emotions free of negativity, this is a glorious state in a magical world. Mythically, this is what some mythologists describe as being possessed by a god or filled with a divine elixir.

No one is unchanged by a highly emotional Meeting with the Goddess. Experiences of rebirth are life-transforming events. The mythic adventure of Actaeon is an example of just how dramatic this transformation can be.

> Actaeon chanced to see the dangerous goddess at
> noon; that fateful moment when the sun breaks
> in its youthful, strong ascent, balances, and

begins the mighty plunge to death. He had left his companions to rest, together with his blooded dogs, after a morning of running game, and without conscious purpose had gone wandering, straying from his familiar hunting groves and fields, exploring through the neighboring woods. He discovered a vale, thick grown with cypresses and pine. He penetrated curiously into its fastness. There was a grotto within [sic] in, watered by a gentle, purling spring and with a stream that widened to a grassy pool. This shaded nook was the resort of Diana, and at the moment she was bathing among her nymphs, absolutely naked. She had put aside her hunting spear, her quiver, her unstrung bow, as well as her sandals and her robe. And one of the nude nymphs had bound up her tresses into a knot; some of the others were pouring water from capacious urns.

When the young, roving male broke into the pleasant haunt, a shriek of female terror went up, and all the bodies crowded about their mistress, trying to hide her from the profane eye. But she stood above them, head and shoulders. The youth had seen and was continuing to see. She glanced for her bow, but it was out of reach, so she quickly took up what was at hand, namely water, and flung it into Actaeon's face. "Now you are free to tell, if you can," she cried at him angrily, "that you have seen the goddess nude."

Antlers sprouted on his head. His neck grew great and long, his eartips sharp. His arms lengthened to legs, and his hands and feet became hooves. (Campbell 111-2)

Actaeon happened upon the Goddess at high noon when the sun was at the height of its power. He encountered the Goddess, not in one of her many manifestations where "she reduces her effulgence and permits herself to appear in forms concordant with [his] undeveloped powers."(Campbell 115). Actaeon met with the Goddess in all her naked glory. He experiences a shattering of illusory realities, a blast that completely obliterates his cage of Mythlock. Actaeon is reborn and changed forever.

The Actaeon story stresses how dramatic the transformation of rebirth can be. A hunter is turned into the hunted. Psychologically this could be a transformation of attitude from one who enjoys the thrill of the hunt into a man who finds the senseless killing of animals for sport abhorrent and is beaten up by his hunting buddies for his heresy.

My experience fits this description of a Meeting with the Goddess in all her splendor. My whole world changed. I became a child again and everywhere I looked I discovered something new and exciting, and I just had to share the wonder. I saw the same faults I had discovered in myself in front of The Looking Glass manifest in the behavior of my friends. Foolishly, I pointed this out to them and none of them welcomed the criticism. I escaped the trauma of Actaeon because I had good and very tolerant friends. Regardless of the specifics of the transformation, the impact is a shattering of the veil of Mythlock. This is an experience of rebirth.

A Meeting with the Goddess in all her splendor and glory is ecstatically emotional. When the attempt is made to describe the experience, the images become wildly poetic and beyond empathy.

> Her couch -- and -- throne is there, in a grove
> of wish fulfilling trees. The beaches of the Isle

are of golden sand. They are laved by the still waters of the ocean of the nectar of immortality. The goddess is red with the fire of life; the earth, the solar system, the galaxies of far-extending space, all swell within her womb. For she is the world creatrix, ever mother, ever virgin. She encompasses the encompassing, nourishes the nourishing, and is the life in everything that lives. (Campbell 114)

She is the paragon of all paragons of beauty, the reply to all desire, the bliss-bestowing goal of every hero's earthly and unearthly quest. She is mother, sister, mistress, bride. Whatever in the world has lured, whatever has seemed to promise joy, has been premonitory of her existence -- in the deep of sleep, if not in the cities and forests of the world. For she is the incarnation of the promise of perfection; the soul's assurance that, ... the bliss that once was known will be known again: the comforting, the nourishing, the "good" mother -- young and beautiful -- who was known to us, and even tasted, in the remotest past. Time sealed her away, yet she is dwelling still, like one who sleeps in timelessness, at the bottom of the timeless sea. (Campbell 110-111)

Within our minds, the Goddess is ever-immanent. She waits to bestow upon us our heart's desires.

A Meeting with the Goddess is the source of profound insights of the genius heroes of this world. Herein lies the source of the great philosophies we study in school. Herein lies the source of the world's great religions. The messages of Buddha, Jesus, and Mohammad, while differing in detail, provide a comprehensive understanding that facilitates survival and adaptation. The religions arising from their lives, added to and modified by adherents over the ages, provide structure for organizing society and answers to assist individuals in dealing with the tragedies of life and death.

> '... without the more spectacular exploratory dives of the creative individual, there would be no science and no art' (Koestler 181).

And, there would be no religion. All the world's big ideas are the products of the minds of heroes who undertook a Monomythic Journey.

A Meeting with the Goddess is a high. Once we embrace a new understanding, stability is re-established in our lives. Gone is the chaos of uncertainty and the discomfort that prompted the Adventure in the first place. When we embrace the new understanding, our Monomythic Adventure is complete. But never forget: the Goddess always promises more. If we are not mesmerized by the beauty of the answer discovered, our minds can remain fluid. If we can endure the turbulence of a fluid mind, the inner Adventure may not yet be complete.

The Garden of the Goddess, the realm of the human mind, is a magically fluid realm. In the Garden flowers and fruit trees still in bud can, with the slightest shift of thought open into full bloom right before our eyes. Equally quick, trees in blossom can turn into trees laden with harvest fruits. A cornucopia of fruits and vegetables with another twist of the eye can be transformed into gastronomic delights accompanied by an ample supply of crystal goblets filled with wine. If our minds remain fluid more can come. At the center of the garden, a clear pool reflects the richness of the garden but the image of one reflection quickly catches and holds the eye. There, across the pool, resting lightly on a couch of soft golden cloth, a garland of flowers in her long flowing hair, and dressed in a simple white gown, lay the image of perfection, the unmatchable beauty of the Goddess herself. The Goddess always promises more. As we watch her with our fluid minds, she rises, turns, and parts a silken curtain behind her couch, and we catch a glimpse of The Stairway to the Stars.

Stairway to the Stars

We are the center and the circumference of our own universe.

Mythlock is a reality of the adult world. In childhood, we build a repertoire of knowledge, experience, and beliefs that creates our understanding of the world we inhabit. As children, our brains are wired as we adapt to the familial and cultural environment into which we are born. We become what we behold and in time our responses become habitual, and we behold what we've become. The world we inhabit and all its meaning is a product of our existing understanding. The adaptive strategy we use to interact with the world arises from this understanding. The quality of our lives is dependent upon this understanding.

A Meeting with the Goddess may break us out of Mythlock into a broader and perhaps more comprehensive world but once mesmerized by the beauty of our new understanding we have merely entered a broader and perhaps more adequate cage of Mythlock. Regardless of what cage we inhabit, the metric for measuring the quality of our adaptive strategy, or the quality of the myths of our minds, is how happy we are with our lives.

We are the authors of our lives. The world we perceive is a creation of our own making. The pessimist, for example, firmly believes that the world is an ugly, violent, malevolent place. The feelings incorporated in this belief call forth unconscious, habitual, myths of the mind, which aroused similar feelings in the past. Using these myths, the conscious mind is drawn, like a magnet, to incidents that confirm this belief, and contrary evidence is effectively filtered out. Again, and again this belief is confirmed. The motivation of the conscious mind is to make us feel good and it always feels good to be proven right. As a result, the pessimist inhabits an ugly, violent, malevolent world with most of its beauty filtered out.

The optimist, on the other hand, believes that the world is a beautiful place filled with caring individuals. Again, the feelings engendered by this belief call forth myths of the mind that aroused similar feelings in the past. Using these myths, the optimist's conscious mind is drawn, like a magnet, to incidents in the world that confirm this belief. Again, and again this belief is confirmed. The motivation of the conscious mind is to make us feel good and it always feels good to be proven right. As a result, the optimist inhabits a beautiful world filled with caring individuals with most of the viciousness filtered out.

We inhabit a world of our own creation.

> We become what we behold and
> we behold what we've become.

If you think about it for a moment, pessimists are foolish because they choose to inhabit an ugly, violent, malevolent world and contrary evidence that might reveal a beautiful world, is filtered out. The fact is, of course, that the world encompasses all. It is actually wiggly lines whether we perceive faces or a vase. There are those who class themselves as neither optimist nor pessimist. They declare themselves realists. Realists look the world straight in the eye, enjoy its beauty and never flinch from the grosser realities of life. They do not wear rose-colored glasses to hide the often ugly, violent, and malevolent events in the world. They are realists! Realists believe that it is possible to observe the world through objective eyes. They are unaware that the myths of their minds create all the meaning they perceived and filter out information irrelevant to the meaning they create. Realists are deluded because they believe that objective observation is possible. The fact is that the perception of objective reality is beyond the capability of the human perceptual organs. All that reaches the mind is the raw data of the senses. There is no meaning except that imparted to the raw data of our senses by the dominant myths of our minds.

Our habitual responses arise from the meaning created by the invisible myths of our minds and not all our habits lead to positive results. Based upon unrecognized misunderstandings or faulty myths, we may have an incorrect understanding of the reality of the world around us. Or the world we live in could change rendering old habitual responses inadequate in the new environment. Our response in these situations may not lead to the results we desire. When we encounter a situation that matters to us where our existing adaptive response fails, we face a crisis of adaptation. Discomfort or disruption enters our lives. We need to undertake a Monomythic Journey; we need to use our innate creative potential to look at the situation in a new light to reveal new information; so, we can come up with a new understanding and devise a new adaptive strategy. This is how it works or how it should work and probably does for those people who lead successful, happy lives. But this is not how it happens for the majority of us. For most of us:

> The future is regarded not in terms of an unremitting series of deaths and births, but as though one's present system of ideals, virtues, goals and advantages were to be fixed and made secure. (Campbell 60.)

Most of us are firmly caught in the cage of Mythlock and the quality of the cage within which we resided is a measure of how happy we are with our lives.

A Meeting with the Goddess in all her glory shatters our existing cage of Mythlock. It not only breaks us free from the faulty myth causing the crisis, but it liberates us completely from the cage of Mythlock. An Escape from Mythlock is a wildly fluid, highly unstable, and frequently frightening state of mind. Rescue from this unstable and potentially frightening state becomes the immediate goal of the conscious mind. Whether the conscious mind devises its own answer or adopts a comprehensive one ready-made in existing philosophies or religions of the world, adoption is generally quick with the relief magnifying the beauty of the accepted solution. A Meeting with the Goddess may shatter our existing cage of Mythlock but the mesmerizing beauty of the new understanding we gain through the experience can more than compensate. The intensity of the emotions can magnify the beauty creating a sense of certainty impervious to rational evaluation. The experience of rebirth can result in an understanding that creates stability in our lives such that no contrary evidence can shake us from our faith. The adequacy of this new adaptive strategy, again, is how happy we are with our lives.

In the presence of the Goddess, our minds are fluid. If one does not become mesmerized by the beauty of the Goddess, a unique psychological event is possible. It is an event that imparts an understanding of the roles of our conscious mind and our feelings in the act of perception. It is an event that shows that our conscious mind is the author of the meaning we perceive. It is an event that shows that it is our feelings that validate the answer devised. It is an event that provides an understanding of the cycle of Mythlock and the escape from Mythlock as we grow as human beings.

Within the Garden of the Goddess a question arises, and with a new perspective, a gift from the Goddess, the conscious mind devises an answer. If something about the answer does not feel quite right, the conscious mind will reject this first answer and come up with a better answer almost immediately. If this new answer doesn't feel quite right it can be rejected and another one devised. The process can repeat itself many times until an answer is devised that is not rejected. A key thing to realize about the creative process is that although the conscious mind devises the answers, our feelings evaluate the answers devised. This is the last step in the creative act. The beauty of the answer is the criterion in this evaluation process. The more beautiful the answer, the more intense the feelings of pleasure, and the more certain are we that the truth has been discovered. Within the emotionally fluid Garden of the Goddess, until an answer is devised and accepted, the conscious mind is kept busy just trying to keep up and make sense of all the wonder around it.

There is a wonderful Irish tale of the Prince of Lonesome Isle which follows the entire Monomythic Adventure from the initiating problem to a Meeting with the Goddess in all her splendor. It is a unique tale in that it also includes an ascent up the Stairway to the Stars but without the usual mind-blowing climax. It's as if this Prince is so familiar with the Monomythic Adventure that he just relaxes to the wonder of it all.

> In the west of Ireland, they still tell the tale of the Prince of Lonesome Isle and the Lady of Tubber Tintye. Hoping to heal the Queen of Erin, the heroic youth had undertaken to go for three bottles of water of Tubber Tintye, the flaming fairy well. Following the advice of a supernatural aunt whom he encountered on the way, and riding a wonderful, dirty, lean little shaggy horse that she gave him, he crossed a river of fire and

escaped the touch of a grove of poison trees. The horse with the speed of the wind shot past the end of the castle of Tubber Tintye; the prince sprang from its back through an open window, and came down inside, safe and sound.

"The whole place, enormous in extent, was filled with sleeping giants and monsters of sea and land -- great whales, long slippery eels, bears, and beasts of every form and kind. The prince passed through them and over them till he came to a great stairway. At the head of the stairway he went into a chamber, where he found the most beautiful woman he had ever seen, stretched on a couch asleep. 'I have nothing to say to you,' thought he, and went on to the next; and so he looked into twelve chambers. In each was a woman more beautiful that the one before. But when he reached the thirteenth chamber and opened the door, the flash of gold took the sight from his eyes. He stood awhile till the sight came back, and then entered. In the great bright chamber was a golden couch, resting on wheels of gold. The wheels turned continually; the couch went round and round, never stopping night or day. On the couch lay the Queen of Tubber Tintye; and if her twelve maidens were beautiful, they would not be beautiful if seen next to her. At the foot of the couch was Tubber Tintye itself -- the well of fire. There was a golden cover upon the well, and it went around continually with the couch of the Queen.

"'Upon my word,' said the prince, 'I'll rest here awhile.' And he went up on the couch and never left it for six days and nights." (Campbell 109-10)

The Garden of the Goddess, the realm of the human mind, is "enormous in extent, ... filled with ... giants and monsters" as well as the most beautiful visions imaginable. Up the stairway, each chamber reveals for the Prince an even more beautiful vision than the last until he encounters the Goddess herself.

The mythic tale of the Prince of Lonesome Isle tells the story of an adventure that leads to a Meeting with the Goddess in all her glory. The unique addition is the ascent up the stairway leading from one beautiful vision to ever more beautiful and comprehensive visions. This mythic tale delineates the roles of the conscious mind and our feelings in the creative process when we are within the Garden and our minds are fluid. The Garden is enormous in extent and filled with whatever our imaginations can conjure, giants or monsters or visions of beauty. With all these resources our conscious mind goes to work to devise an understanding that will reintroduce stability. When the answer is devised, it is presented to our feelings for evaluation. We enter the first chamber, and our first answer is like a beautiful woman before our eyes. Or a beautiful man if you're a woman. But if for some reason our feelings are not quite satisfied or we yearn for more, our conscious mind dismisses the answer and devises a new and hopefully more adequate answer and presents it to our feelings for approval. Mythically we continue up the stairs to the next chamber and an even more beautiful woman lying on a couch. If again the answer does not feel totally satisfactory, it too is dismissed and symbolically we proceed up the stairway to the next chamber. This process continues until an answer is found that feels just right. Beauty is the measure of evaluation of these understandings. Once content with the understanding devised, we feel that the truth is finally known. In the Prince's tale, he rejects all answers until he encounters the Goddess herself or in this case the Queen of Tubber Tintye.

If we accept the first solution devised, we will still feel as if the truth is finally known. Our conscious mind does not care which answer is accepted because the goal of the conscious mind is merely the elimination of the feelings of discomfort, which is achieved when our feelings accept an answer.

The tale of the Prince of Lonesome Isle illustrates a mind in the wild throes of creativity. A fluid mind can devise and dismiss answers so fast it can have your head spinning. The Prince's ascent up the stairway from vision to ever more beautiful vision is a reflection of this process. In the tale, the Prince finally experiences a Meeting with the Goddess in all her glory. But unlike a Meeting with the Goddess that shatters the cage of Mythlock and bestows upon us a new perspective, the Prince's mind is already free from Mythlock before he meets the Goddess. What our Prince may not know, although his relaxed behavior hints that he may have experienced it already in the past, is that at the top of the Stairway to the Stars lies the most mind-blowing experience possible for any Monomythic Adventurer, Nirvana.

The dictionary defines Nirvana as literally, "a blowing out" and this is the blowing away of all boundaries. It is a blowing of the mind. An additional definition says that Nirvana is the state of complete blessedness attained when the individual soul is absorbed into and united with, the divine infinity, and all personality is extinguished (Universal Dictionary 776). The emotions of the experience are so wonderful that only religious hyperbole comes close to describing it. This is the experience inherent in a vision from the top of the Stairway to the Stars.

The Goddess always promises more; beyond the Goddess lies the Stairway to the Stars. Imagine a grand inverted Stairway, narrow at its base, with each step it widens, the next step wider than the one before and the next wider yet, as it twists and turns like a ribbon of stairs rising upward into a galaxy of stars. This is my image of the Stairway to the Stars. Up this stairway lies the ultimate experience of the Monomythic Adventure. A mind in the throes of creativity is a mind ripe for an ascent up the Stairway to the Stars. Images used by those who have had this experience and attempted to communicate its essence become so fantastic that they defy comprehension. Can you imagine the ecstasy, in the reality of human emotional response, that lies within the word, Nirvana? It defies comprehension because the experience is an inner emotional experience communicable only through fantastic images. It is an experience of pure feeling.

I am going to try the impossible. I am going to try to communicate a reality-based, psychological description of an ascent up the Stairway to the Stars. Following are the thoughts and ideas that precipitated my own experience of an ascent up the Stairway to the Stars.

Imagine a beautiful day in early summer. Everything is green; the rich green of spring and flowers are blooming in the garden. The sky is crystal blue with white puffy clouds floating by. You are resting on a deck, luxuriating in the warmth of the sun, contemplating life. You think about all your friends and relatives who despite all their differences, minor maladaptations, and idiosyncrasies, are at heart, warm, caring, and compassionate individuals. How fortunate you are to have these people as friends. A warm feeling of love flows through your body. Suddenly you realize you are being too selective as the image of a stranger's child flashes through your mind. You see this child playing on the lawn, smiling in wide-eyed wonder. All children, you realize, are beautiful just like your friends. The joy embedded in these thoughts washes through your body, heightening your emotions and unknowingly you take a step up the Stairway to the Stars. Suddenly images of other people you know and even strangers flash through your mind and their smiles warm your heart. You are still being too selective. Taking another step up the Stairway to the Stars, you realize that all people are beautiful. Then immediately, as if to correct a misconception, the image of a rough, tough, leather-jacketed biker flashes through your mind, as if to point out a fallacy. But you watch him become a hesitant, bashful little boy in the presence of a beautiful woman. You see him sitting awkwardly playing tentatively with a child in his lap, tenderness, and caring filling his eyes. You see through the veneer of the conscious constructs buffering his inner child from the outer world. Within every human being, just below the public veneer of conscious adaptation is a beautiful, fragile child. All people are beautiful.

Regardless of race, religion, or culture, beneath the veneer of differences, lies a beautiful fragile human being with all the same hopes, dreams, and desires as yourself. The wonder and awe of this revelation fills your heart to bursting and you take yet another step up the Stairway to the Stars. Then a golden retriever, lying at your feet, turns and looks up at you with those big brown eyes. You are still being far too selective. Your golden retriever is beautiful. Suddenly, you see that all nature's animals are beautiful as you watch a hummingbird hover at the blossom of a foxglove. You take another step up the Stairway to the Stars. Everything alive is beautiful; life is beautiful. A shot of ecstasy fills your eyes with tears of joy as you take yet another step up the Stairway to the Stars.

You pause a moment and remember hearing somewhere that there is more similarity between the DNA structure of a tree and a human being than there are differences. It's not just animals, but everything alive is beautiful. You become absorbed in the beauty of the soft mauve petal of an iris blooming in the garden and you take yet another step up the Stairway to the Stars. Another thought pops into your fluid mind. You are still being too selective. You remember the words of Carl Sagan, "We are the stuff of stars." Everything we know, and out of which life has evolved, is created in the burning cauldron of a star and scattered across the universe when a star explodes. We are all, all animals, all plants, all living things, and even the soil, water, air, and the very mountains, made of the stuff of stars. We are all of one. The wonder and awe of this emotional revelation cause every cell in your body to tingle. Tears of joy pour down your face. You feel tingling in your fingertips like lines of force extending outward and connecting to all around you. Every cell in your body tingles with its own lines of force connecting everything to everything. All is one! You are a part of everything and everything is a part of you. The ecstasy of this revelation burns your eyes with tears as your "soul is absorbed into, and united with, the divine infinity and all personality is extinguished."

You are not separate; you are not alone. You are a part of all and all is a part of you. You are one with the universe. This is the penultimate possible experience of a Monomythic Adventure. Feeling the oneness of all. It is an indescribable ecstasy. Even the lessons learned can only be expressed in poetry.

> For every aspect of life, we reject
> We increase the paucity of our existence.
> For every aspect of life, we absorb
> We enrich our lives.

Every step up the Stairway to the Stars expands the horizons of our world and enriches our lives.

From the top of the Stairway to the Stars, you can see forever. Our horizon is expanded to the limitless boundaries of eternity. We can observe the universe unfolding as it should according to the law and nature of its being. This is a perspective beyond boundaries. This is a god or goddess-like perspective. This is life seen through the lens of eternity.

> From the standpoint of the Olympians, eon after eon of earthly history rolls by, revealing ever the harmonious form of the total round, so that where men see only change and death, the blessed behold immutable form, world without end. (Campbell 223)

This is the meaning behind the words of Walt Whitman:

> I laugh at what you call dissolution;
> I know the amplitude of time.
> (Walt Whitman 84-85)

From the perspective of eternity, failure, disaster, and even the most crushing tragedies become merely bumps on the road of existence.

An ascent up the Stairway to the Stars is the most exotic potentiality of any revelatory experience. Because it is so emotional, so personal and so beyond the normal, it is impossible to communicate its reality in any accurate way. Any description is filled with hyperbole. Imagine seeing protons of light from the sun striking and being absorbed by the leaves of the trees. Imagine seeing the colors of the rainbow bouncing off shiny surfaces everywhere. This might be explained as an existential experience of the direct perception of the raw data of our senses without any intervening organization imposed by the myths of our minds or just an unfettered imagination playing havoc with our visual senses. Then again, imagine the feelings behind the image of dissolving and becoming one with the universe. Imagine feeling the interconnectedness of all things. Imagine emotionally experiencing the meaning of the words, all is one. The creative act is the adaptive response and an ascent up the Stairway to the Stars is the ultimate potential of the creative act.

But what adaptive advantage lies in such an exotic experience? As the ultimate experience of a Monomythic Adventure, it provides an ultimate adaptive advantage. Each step up the Stairway to the Stars lead the Prince of Lonesome Isle from one beautiful woman to an ever more beautiful woman until he encountered the unmatchable beauty of the Goddess herself. Each step up the stairway led to a broader, more comprehensive, and more inclusive vision than the last. The conscious process depicted in this image is the rejection of one perspective and the adoption of one that is broader and more comprehensive. The conscious process described by the image of an ascent up the Stairway to the Stars is generalization and generalization is a powerful means of expanding the potential of any perspective to provide a more inclusive understanding.

Take, for example, the idea inherent in the words, "Boston marathon race." The idea inherent in these words describes a specific type of race that takes place at a specific time every year and in a specific place. By generalizing it to "marathon race" it now has application to a specific type of race, which can take place anywhere, anytime. Further, generalize it to the word "race" and the perspective inherent in the word can now create understanding to five people standing in a row, ten people perched on the edge of a swimming pool, fifteen horses behind a gate, and even four frogs under a barrel. In all these cases this simple perspective inherent in the word "race," provides meaning and understanding to the contents of these situations. The power of a generalized perspective is its ability to provide understanding in a wide variety of situations. Generalization is a powerful tool of the conscious mind and a significantly powerful strategy when it comes to the Escape from Mythlock.

Gaining a new perspective is the essence of any inspirational experience. Gaining a broader perspective is the essence of any ascent up the Stairway to the Stars. Being trapped in a narrow perspective or confining myth of the mind is often the source of a crisis. A teenager is dumped by his girlfriend. Madly in love, open and vulnerable, and suddenly his world is devastated. His life becomes empty and devoid of meaning and his world dark and depressing. He beholds what he's become. Life is no longer worth living. Suicide becomes an option. Escape from this limiting myth of the mind becomes essential for his survival. We advise him to put the situation in perspective. We tell him that in a year the crisis will be forgotten. We tell him that in five years he will have forgotten her name. We try to use the perspective of time to diminish the emotional impact of the trauma of the moment. If we fail to succeed our teenager is still in danger. If the teenager fails to broaden his perspective, he or she is still in danger.

This broadening of perspective is a critical adaptive strategy. It can rescue us from any precipitous and disastrous decisions arising out of a desperate struggle to escape from Mythlock. The ability to generalize our perspective is a key to the cage of Mythlock. This key is a gift to any Adventurer who experiences an ascent up the Stairway to the Stars. Trapped in Mythlock, these heroes know to step back, see the situation from a broader perspective and escape. They know to proceed up the Stairway to the Stars to a broader perspective. This is an adaptive strategy burnt into the minds of these Adventurers. From the top of the Stairway to the Stars, we can see eternity and become forever immune to the dangers of the trap of Mythlock. This is no small adaptive advantage.

What is the final trigger for an inspirational event? Locked in the sticky tar of Mythlock, suddenly we somehow break out and gain a new perspective that casts new light on the situation. We know that feelings of discomfort are an incentive. Could this emotional discomfort have as its goal nothing more than forcing us to broaden our perspective? One step up the Stairway to the Stars is a rejection of one perspective and the adoption of a newer and broader perspective. Could the source of the magic moment of any inspirational experience be nothing more than the adoption of a broader perspective? Could the act of generalization be the secret of the magic moment of inspiration? This rational explanation may appear to diminish some of the magic of the inspirational moment but not really. The excitement of the moment of inspiration is an emotional moment and a rational explanation cannot diminish the awe of the experience itself.

From the top of the Stairway to the Stars, you can see forever. This is the ultimate perspective, the ultimate generalization – all is one. There is no confusion. This is the experience that leads the guru on the mountaintop to proclaim, 'The universe is unfolding as it should.' This perspective is also the ultimate rose-colored glasses. The universe may be unfolding according to the law and nature of its being, but the world of man is not unfolding as it should. If it was, we would inhabit paradise. The guru who sits atop his mountain declaring that "The universe is unfolding as it should," is a Monomythic Adventurer who has yet to face the greatest challenge. The greatest challenge for any Monomythic Adventurer is the Challenge of the Return. The real heroes of life and mythology are those who accept the Challenge of the Return -- to make their vision a shared vision, to make their dream a shared dream, to make the wonders of their imagined world within, manifest in the world without. This is the Challenge of the Return where real heroes are forged in the crucible of reality.

The Crucible of Reality

The Challenge of the Return

Wisdom is keeping uppermost in mind the ultimate goal of the Monomythic Journey - 'to live happily ever after'.

Within the Garden of the Goddess, the mind is fluid, and we feel everything. We feel more alive than we could ever have imagined possible. The grass is greener; the flowers smell sweeter, and just a smile from another human being can fill the heart to bursting. The mind races, everything has meaning. This is paradise. Cleansed of any feelings of guilt, regret, or anger and liberated from the tyranny of fear, this is heaven. But we cannot reside forever within the Garden of the Goddess. We cannot live our lives solely within the virtual world of our minds.

> When the hero-quest has been accomplished, through penetration to the source, or the grace of some male or female, human or animal, personification, the adventurer still must return with his life-transmuting trophy. The full round, the norm of the monomyth, requires that the hero shall now begin the labor of bringing the runes of wisdom, the Golden Fleece, or his sleeping princess, back into the kingdom of humanity, where the boon may redound to the renewing of the community, the nation, the planet, or the ten thousand worlds. (Campbell 193)

Whether a grandiose revitalization of the world, surviving a crisis or making a dream come true, when the inner adventure ends the Challenge of the Return begins. This is where success or failure of the Monomythic Journey is determined. In the more grandiose events, this is the part of the hero's story that makes the history books.

Within the Garden of the Goddess, the mind is in a fluid state, and enthusiasm, an emotion of creativity is rampant. This is the norm within the Garden. Enthusiasm is a primary outer manifestation of the inner creative spirit. The word itself is derived from 'the god or goddess within.' Enthusiasm is to be possessed by a god or goddess. But maintaining the fluidity of mind, engendered within the Garden of the Goddess in the face of all the petty concerns of every day is next to impossible and most often, a fruitless endeavor.

Sir James George Frazer in his book, The Golden Bough, lists countless myths and folktales from around the world, which illustrate the nature of this challenge.

> Sir James George Frazer explains in the following graphic way the fact that over the whole earth, the divine personage may not touch the ground with his foot. Apparently, holiness, magical virtue, taboo, or whatever we may call that mysterious quality that is supposed to pervade sacred or tabooed persons, is conceived by the primitive philosopher as a physical substance or fluid, with which the sacred man is charged just as a Leyden jar is charged with electricity; and exactly as the electricity in the jar can be discharged by contact with a good conductor, so the holiness or magical virtue in the man can be discharged and drained away by contact with the earth, which on this

theory serves as an excellent conductor for the magical fluid. Hence to preserve the charge from running to waste, the sacred or tabooed personage must be carefully prevented from touching the ground; in electrical language, he must be insulated, if he is not to be emptied of the precious substance or fluid with which he, as a vial, is filled to the brim. (Campbell 224-5)

The "primitive philosophers" may call this magical and mysterious fluid, holiness, but fluidity of mind is the psychological reality. This fluidity of mind engenders excitement and enthusiasm, the dominant emotions of the returning adventurer. Frazer's idea of the Leyden jar and the grounding out of an electrical charge is a very apropos metaphor.

The experience of being grounded out like the charge in a Leyden jar is common. Children inhabit the Garden. Watch what happens to a child, excited by some discovery, who comes to share their boon with a busy adult. You can see the hurt in the young child's eyes when their enthusiasm is rebuffed or crushed by an inappropriate response. Enthusiasm is a delicate flower easily crushed.

During my months of Monomythic Adventure, I was on a high. My mind was fluid and my enthusiasm unbounded. I loved seeing things from a new perspective because of the shot of pleasure that comes with inspiration. I loved exploring new ideas and I could see profound implications in the most mundane. I was also not at all hesitant to share these profound insights with my friends, whether they wanted to hear them or not.

I remember one friend throwing his hands in the air one-day exclaiming, "Can't we just talk about football anymore?" Endless profundity, it seems, can become tedious. A fluid mind is wonderfully exciting for a person with a fluid mind. For others, the constant enthusiasm can in time become an irritant. At the time I was too engrossed to notice the negative impact I was having on others. When I finally realized what I was doing to my friends, I immediately ceased. I remember the exact moment. This was also, unknown to me at the time, the exact moment the inner portion of my adventure ended when my foot touched the soil and my fluidity of mind leached out like the charge from a Leyden jar.

One morning when I entered the Torque Room, the student coffee shop, I noticed a friend put his hand to his forehead and turn away and whisper, "Oh no here he comes again!" Although my eyes may have been opened to many things during my experience, I had not noticed the impact my behavior was having on my friends. I think they thought I had lost my mind. My mind was still fluid and after hearing this whispered comment I immediately realized what was happening. I had become a black cloud of seriousness always dampening the lighthearted banter of the group. I had become obnoxious and vowed immediately to change my behavior. Little did I know the price that I would pay. My fluidity of mind was grounded out like the charge from a Leyden jar announcing that the inner, Garden, portion of my Adventure was over. Although I didn't turn physically blind, the world lost a great deal of its glitter that day and I did feel older.

To prevent this loss, mythological precautions are proscribed.

> The idea of the insulating horse, to keep the hero
> out of immediate touch with the earth and yet
> permit him to promenade among the peoples of

the world, is a vivid example of a basic precaution taken generally by the carriers of supernormal power. (Campbell 224)

But in mythic terms, you can't live a very productive life from the back of a horse. You could become a hermit to isolate yourself from the grounding out concerns of every day. Again, this seems less than an ideal way of living. Or, if you grounded out you could follow the path of Narcissus, and beat yourself black and blue to reinitiate a fluid state of mind. Again, this seems less than ideal. Or you could realize like the Masters of Two Worlds realize, that fluidity of mind is not conducive to survival in the real world and that the fluidity of mind, inspiration, will return, if necessary, when faced with another challenge. Maintaining the fluidity of mind engendered by a visit to the Garden of the Goddess, in a world of every day is almost impossible and not conducive to 'living happily ever after'.

The wonderful Irish tale about Oisin, a Fenian hero, illustrates this loss and mentions another challenge that must be faced.

> Oisin, the son of Finn MacCool, one day was out hunting with his men in the woods of Erin, when he was approached by the daughter of the King of the Land of Youth. Oisin's men had gone ahead with the day's kill, leaving their master with his three dogs to shift for himself. And the mysterious being had appeared to him with the beautiful body of a woman, but the head of a pig. She declared that the head was due to a Druidic spell, promising that it would vanish the very minute he would marry her. "Well, if that is the state you are in," said he, "and if marriage with

175

me will free you from the spell, I'll not leave the pig's head on you long."

Without delay, the pig's head was dispatched and they set out together for Tir na n-Og, the Land of Youth. Oisin dwelt there as a king many happy years. But one day he turned and declared to his supernatural bride: "'I wish I could be in Erin to-day to see my father and his men.'

"'If you go,' said his wife, 'and set foot on the land of Erin, you'll never come back here to me, and you'll become a blind old man. How long do you think it is since you came here?'

"'About three years.' said Oisin.

"'It is three hundred years.' said she, 'since you came to this kingdom with me. If you must go to Erin, I'll give you this white steed to carry you; but if you come down from the steed or touch the soil of Erin with your foot, the steed will come back that minute, and you'll be where he left you, a poor old man.'

"'I'll come back, never fear,' said Oisin. 'Have I not good reason to come back? But I must see my father and my son and my friends in Erin once more; I must have even one look at them.'

"She prepared the steed for Oisin and said, 'The steed will carry you wherever you wish to go.'

"Oisin never stopped till the steed touched the soil of Erin; and he went on till he came to Knock

Patrick in Munster, where he saw a man herding cows. In the field where the cows were grazing there was a broad flat stone.

"'Will you come here,' said Oisin to the herdsman, 'and turn over this stone?'

"'Indeed, then, I will not,' said the herdsman; 'for I could not lift it, nor twenty men more like me.'

"Oisin rode up to the stone, and reaching down, caught it with his hand and turned it over. Underneath the stone was the great horn of the Fenians (borabu), which circled round like a seashell, and it was the rule that when any of the Fenians of Erin blew the borabu, the others would assemble at once from whatever part of the country they might be in at the time.

"'Will you bring this horn to me?' asked Oisin of the herdsman.

"'I will not,' said the herdsman; 'for neither I nor many more like me could raise it from the ground.'

With that Oisin moved near the horn and reaching down took it in his hand; but so eager was he to blow it, that he forgot everything, and slipped in reaching till one foot touched the earth. In an instant the steed was gone, and Oisin lay on the ground a blind old man." (Campbell 221-3)

Oisin was eager, excited, and enthusiastic about seeing his father and friends again. But when his foot touched the ground all the vitality he possessed was drained away leaving nothing but a blind old man.

The grounding out of a fluid mind is not the only Challenge of the Return illustrated by the Oisin tale. When Oisin is asked how long he believes he has dwelt in Tir na n-Og, he says, 'three years.' only to find out it has been three hundred years. Within the Garden of the Goddess time is malleable. Within the Garden, you can watch a whole lifetime pass in the flash of an eye. You can see a dream born, struggle for life, mature, and manifest itself in full in the flash of an eye. But in the world of every day, it takes a lifetime for a lifetime to flash by. Within the world of every day, it can take, days, months, or even years for a dream to be made a reality. Time is different within the realm of the mind.

> The equating of a single year in Paradise to one hundred of earthly existence is a motif well-known to myth. The full round of one hundred signifies totality. Similarly, the three hundred and sixty degrees of the circle signify totality; accordingly, the Hindu Puranas represent one year of the gods as equal to three hundred and sixty of men. (Campbell 223)

Within the Garden of the Goddess, time can go forward, backward, fast, or slow because this is the realm of all possibilities. But within the world of every day, a second takes a second to pass, a minute takes a minute, a day, a day and a year, a full year to go by. The young entrepreneur with a new product idea, working the figures out on his calculator, projecting costs, profit per unit, and sales volume expected and in the flash of an eye, he sees himself a millionaire sitting on a South Sea Island sipping Pina Coladas through a straw. In the real world, it can take a little longer to make a dream come true. The reality of time is another challenge facing the returning hero.

We see singers, dancers, and actors who have achieved success. We do not see the years of struggle preceding this success. We do not see the failures and setbacks that crushed their spirit, the times their enthusiasm waned, the times they were ready to give up. We hear about overnight successes, which reminds me of an interview with a musician whose popularity had just blossomed. When asked about his overnight success he responded, 'Yes, it only took me forty years to become an overnight success.' Maintaining the enthusiasm engendered by a visit to the Garden of the Goddess in the face of everyday concerns is one challenge faced by the returning hero. Maintaining the drive and persevering in the face of the interminable slowness of time required to make dreams come true is another. But, these are only two of the more benign Challenges of the Return.

The Cassandra Syndrome

Not until a new perspective is put on like a pair of sunglasses and used to create new meaning to events in the world around us, are the full implications understood. Not until a new perspective is emotionally absorbed is there understanding.

Enthusiasm is the outer manifestation of an inner, fluid, creative mental state. Regardless of the contents of the thought, when enthusiasm has us in its grasp, we inhabit the Garden of the Goddess. Accompanying this enthusiastic exuberance is a natural tendency to want to share the joy. This can be experienced with even the simplest of inspirational events. We discover a solution to a troublesome math problem and bubbling with excitement we share the joys of our discovery with those around us. They look at the solution we offer and respond, "Of course, that's how you do it. Everyone knows that!" Apparently in this instance, what is new to us turns out to be old hat to others. Our enthusiasm leeches out like the charge in a grounded Leyden jar. Although in this instance we may not have been able to share our joy, we were, at least, able to make them understand what we were talking about. This is not always the case.

There is a mythological character named Cassandra who is constantly exposed to this frustration of communication. Cassandra was given the gift of prophecy by a god but because she reneged on her part of the bargain, the gift was modified so that when she told the future, nobody could understand a thing she was saying. She predicted the fall of Troy but all who might have done something about it couldn't understand a thing she was saying. She watched in knowing anguish, horror, and frustration as all that she said came true. Cassandra was a prophet who could see the future but was unable to get others to see what she saw.

There are Cassandras all over the place. Years ago, a scientist or maybe a group of scientists speculated that the increasing output of hydrocarbons by our modern industrial complex could raise the temperature of the world. They speculated on the potentially disastrous impact in the future of major global climate change. They invented the term Global Warming. But tell someone bundled up against the wind in minus 20-degree weather, that the earth is warming up and the idea seems a little far-fetched. Seeing the future is pure speculation and very hard to find concrete everyday examples to help convince the skeptics. It turns out that the twentieth century was the warmest in recorded history. In some of the latter years, the world experienced some of the warmest years on record. Of course, on a global scale, the actual temperature change is small. Now again, tell someone who experiences minus 20-degree weather in the winter and high 30s in the summer that a few degrees of global temperature change are significant. Not until there are torrential rains where rain is generally moderate, droughts where moisture is usually adequate and storms of unprecedented violence and frequency, will the Cassandras of global warming have concrete evidence for the future they have foreseen. These days we are seeing torrential rains, droughts, and storms of unprecedented violence and frequency. Global warming is a fact and we had better get working to mitigate its impact.

Failure to communicate ideas that we feel are critically important can lead to disappointment and even despair in our returning adventurer. This happens in all areas of human endeavors and in some instances the results are tragic.

> The martyrology of science mentions only a few conspicuous cases, which ended in public tragedies. Robert Mayer, co-discoverer of the Principle of the Conservation of Energy, went insane because of a lack of recognition for his work. So did Ignaz Semmelweiss, who discovered, in 1847, that the cause of childbed fever was infection of the patient with the 'cadaveric material' which surgeons and students carried on their hands. As an assistant at the General Hospital in Vienna, Semmelweiss introduced the strict rule of washing hands in chlorinated lime water before entering the ward. Before his innovation, one out of every eight women in the ward had died of puerperal fever; immediately afterwards mortality fell to one in thirty, and the next year to one in a hundred. Semmelweiss's reward was to be hounded out of Vienna by the medical professions -- which was moved, apart from stupidity, by resentment of the suggestion that they might be carrying death on their hands. He went to Budapest, but made little headway with his doctrine, denounced his opponents as murderers, became raving mad, was put into a restraining jacket, and died in a mental hospital. (Koestler 239-240)

I can imagine Semmelweiss, arrogantly propounding his idea that the doctors were carrying death on their hands and then calling them idiots and murderers when they refused to accept his explanation. Blaming the failure of others to understand for our failure to communicate is simply Scapegoatism.

Calling people idiots and murderers is definitely a failure to communicate and the response to this inappropriate method of communication is predictable. How would you respond to some arrogant, self-righteous person calling you an idiot and murderer? Quite simply, you would run him out of Vienna. Failure often results when the returning adventurer does not realize that the frustration arising out of the challenge of communications is merely a harbinger of the need for yet another Monomythic excursion to find a way around the new difficulty.

The result of a successful inspirational event is a new way of looking at things. Whether using this new perspective to devise a simple solution to a simple problem, resolve a major mystery, or revitalize our lives, the result of any inspirational or revelatory experience is always the acquisition of a new perspective. Using the new information revealed by the new perspective, our conscious minds devise a new understanding, a new myth of the mind. If the insight from the inspirational event leads to the development of a new understanding of the reality-based contents of the world, for example, a new theory in science, we face the challenge of standard communications. While never easy, the process is straightforward. The goal is to communicate a new way of looking at specific, external, reality-based contents.

But even in scientific endeavors, and even if our explanation is prepared according to all the precepts of a discipline, the response received is hardly ever, wild applause and enthusiastic acceptance. This is a new idea and new ideas are the "fastest-acting antigen known to science" (Koestler 216). Existing theories, firmly ensconced in the minds of colleagues, are tenacious in self-preservation. How would it feel to have your life's work rendered insignificant because another scientist comes up with a new idea? The scientist with a new theory can find himself or herself under attack, ridiculed, and even scorned. If the new theory has any value, and there are no guarantees, it may eventually be accepted.

The basic challenge of communicating any new idea is the need to pass on a new way of looking at things. Even if the contents are external, observable facts, it is not until the idea is absorbed that the message becomes clear and obvious. Not until the new perspective is put on like a pair of sunglasses are the often radical and exciting implications manifest. Those looking through different perceptual filters see differently, and their myths of the mind filter out information critical to seeing the implications of the new idea. What the purveyors of a new idea see as obvious, others can fail to see at all.

We all view the world through the myths of our minds, which give rise to the meaning we perceive and tend to filter out information irrelevant to the meaning they create. With another perceptual filter looking at the same contents, we can see a different meaning, which again tends to filter out irrelevant information to the meaning it creates. If we look at the picture one way, we see two faces. If we look at the picture another way, we see a vase. It is impossible to see both at the same time. Every act of perception is governed by this reality. Every act of communication is governed by this same reality. Here in lies a major challenge of the Return.

We can use reality-based objects, images, metaphors, or whatever content is appropriate to present an idea. But the meaning and implications of all those objects, images, and metaphors arise from the myths residing within the mind of the listener. If the person to whom we are explaining the new idea is using a different myth or perspective, he or she may perceive meaning differently from the meaning we intend. While we are describing faces, they may be seeing a vase and wondering what the hell we are talking about. Explaining a 'demonstrable hypothesis rationally founded on observable fact' (Campbell 33-34) is one challenge but explaining an inner, non-observable, emotionally charged concept takes the problem to another plane.

This challenge of communication affects most returning heroes. The Parable of the Sower from Christian mythology is Jesus's attempt to describe this communication challenge.

> A sower went out to sow. And as he sowed, some seeds fell along the footpath; and the birds came and ate it up. Some seed fell on rocky ground, where it had little soil, and it sprouted quickly because it had no depth of earth; but when the sun rose the young corn was scorched, and as it had no root it withered away. Some seed fell among thistles, and the thistles shot up and choked the corn. And some seeds fell into good soil, where it bore fruit, yielding a hundredfold or, it might be, sixtyfold or thirtyfold. (Matt 13:3-9)

Although it is generally agreed that the Parable of the Sower is not merely a lesson in horticulture, this is valid content for the pattern delineated by the parable. If we want to be successful in planting seeds, follow the precepts laid out in the parable and success can be ours. Plant good seeds in good soil and the chances are we will succeed.

Another more traditional content for the pattern inherent in the story is to equate the seeds to the words of Jesus and the resulting impact upon his listeners. Sometimes the words were never listened to, and nothing happened. Sometimes the words were received with wild enthusiasm but because they were not absorbed, their implications were not fully understood, and the enthusiasm quickly waned. In other cases, the ideas conflicted with existing, cherished beliefs so the new idea was quickly choked off and rejected. In some cases, the words were heard, fully understood, embraced like Niall embraced the ugly Hag, and the listener could see the implications of Christ's words and went off to share his discovery with others, and the message spread. Jesus used symbolic communications because he was communicating a perspective, a way of looking at things, specifically with the Parable of the Sower, the inner workings of the mind during communications.

The Parable of the Sower illustrates the success or failure of a returning hero to share his or her boon. If a mythic story is heard or read by someone without any thought or investment of emotional effort, the story bounces off like seeds falling on a footpath. This is a simple case of a listener making no effort to try to understand what is being communicated. In some cases, the mythic story is heard and understood and creates meaning to a single specific context or set of circumstances in the mind of the listener. This is seeing Jesus' parable as instructions for the planting of seeds to have a good harvest. While the initial enthusiasm may be high, once a single, final, definitive interpretation is applied and accepted as the only valid interpretation, the communication is over. It goes nowhere after that. The new perspective is applied in one instance. The seed springs up but it has no depth. It hasn't been truly absorbed, put on like sunglasses, so it withers away. This happens when myths are interpreted literally.

In some cases, the meaning devised from the new perspective may be so radically contrary to existing cherished beliefs that it is rejected, choked off, and dies. The listener sees the new idea simply as a threat to existing beliefs and can begin arguing against it before it is fully presented. This can also be the first step to Scapegoatism. In a few fortunate cases the perspective is absorbed, put on like sunglasses, and suddenly new meaning is observed in thirty, sixty, or even a hundred different situations. The perspective is absorbed and used as a new way of looking at a wide variety of different contents. This is the successful communication of a new perspective that facilitates the creation of understanding in a hundred, sixty, or thirty different situations. The Parable of the Sower is Jesus's attempt to show the inner workings of the mind of a listener during communications and to show any returning hero the reality of the challenge that they face trying to share their exciting revelation.

Mythic communication uses images and fantasy as the content to delineate inner psychological patterns of experience. The intention of symbolic communication is to engage the mind and heart of the listener.

> All mythology is studded with symbols, veiled in allegory; the parables of Christ pose riddles that the audience must solve. The intention is not to obscure the message but to make it more luminous by compelling the recipient to work it out by himself -- to re-create it. Hence the message must be handed to him in implied form .... (Koestler 337-8)

The goal is the communication of a new perspective. Mythic communication is a puzzle that is meant to be played with. We play with it until we find relevant content from our own experience that fits the pattern and can be reorganized by the perceptual filter inherent in the story. The perspective needs to be absorbed to initiate new meaning and to reveal new implications to the contents of our experience and the world around us. This is an emotional process.

During the act of perception, our feelings seek out parallel emotional events from our existing repertoire of knowledge and experience, which then springs to mind creating the meaning we perceive. To mine the message of myth and images we need to engage our feelings. The secret is empathy. By empathizing with the emotional pattern inherent in the story, our feelings can retrieve contents from our repertoire of knowledge and experience that aroused similar feelings in the past.

If you have never experience this difficulty with communications you may have experienced it from the listener's point of view. Have you ever started to listen to someone explain something and then lost interest because of the effort required to understand? You have experienced seeds falling on the common footpath. Have you ever listened to someone enthusiastically explain a new idea and immediately understood it in the context of the explanation and wondered what this person was so excited about? You have experienced the application of a new perspective to a single content like a seed springing up quickly but then going nowhere. Have you ever rejected an idea as nonsense even before it was presented? You have experienced the effects of well-watered weeds choking off new growth. I recall lessons in feminism in a rainy cottage that were strangled by my own deep-rooted myths that would not allow any shoots of enlightenment to take hold in this area at that time. Now have you ever listened to someone communicating a new idea and suddenly understood and started to see far-reaching implications to their idea, implications that they have not even mentioned? This is the absorption of a new perspective and it's casting new light on everything you see. This is seeing new meaning in thirty, sixty, or even a hundred different situations depending upon the fluidity of your mind. This is the successful communication of a new idea discovered on a Monomythic Adventure by a returning hero.

The reason that symbolic communication seems so haphazard is that the most important part of the communication rests with the recipient. Not until the recipient has felt the emotional pattern of the story, absorbed the perspective being communicated, and allowed it to provide a new way of looking at the contents of their experience is communication successful. But the full power and potential of mythic communication are still not achieved until the perspective is absorbed and we start to see the new meaning it creates reflected in the world around us. This is the process required to fully mine the messages of mythology.

When trying to communicate the more dramatic or emotional events of a wild revelatory experience, the problem gets even worse. A Meeting with the Goddess in all her splendor and glory is a dramatic emotional moment when we escape the limiting myths of our minds and our minds become fluid. The experience is indescribable. It is a shift from the limiting perspective of an adult mind locked in Mythlock to that of a young child's wide-eyed wonder. How do you describe that and impart anything of the reality of the moment? How do you describe the radically emotional experience of Nirvana, a feeling of being at one with the universe? These experiences take the challenges of mythic communications into another sphere. These are experiences of pure emotion and are almost impossible to communicate because there is no familiar parallel to use as a metaphor.

> How render back into light-world language the speech-defying pronouncements of the dark? How represent on a two-dimensional surface a three-dimensional form, or in a three-dimensional image a multi-dimensional meaning? How translate into terms of "yes" and "no" revelations that shatter into meaninglessness every attempt to define the pairs of opposites? How communicate to people who insist on the

> exclusive evidence of their senses the message of
> the all-generating void? (Campbell 218)

Within the Buddhist tradition, they don't even try.

> The point is that Buddhahood, Enlightenment,
> cannot be communicated, but only the
> way to Enlightenment. This doctrine of the
> incommunicability of the Truth which is beyond
> names and forms is basic to the great Oriental,
> as well as to the Platonic, traditions. Whereas
> the truths of science are communicable, being
> demonstrable hypotheses rationally founded
> on observable facts, ritual, mythology, and
> metaphysics are but guides to the brink of a
> transcendent illumination, the final step to
> which must be taken by each in his own silent
> experience. (Campbell 33-34)

The final step in all symbolic communications is always in the
hands of the recipient. Successful symbolic communication is
beyond the control of the teller of the tale.

The Cassandra Syndrome is a major challenge of the return.
Failure to recognize this reality can lead to disaster as it did
in the lives of Robert Mayer and Ignaz Semmelweiss. This
book is yet another attempt to share the lessons I learned
on my adventure. I wrote a first draft many years ago. The
title was Meeting with the Goddess: Myth, Fairy Tale: Living
Happily Ever After. With the lack of success in getting anyone
to understand what I was trying to say, I started to believe, no
matter what I tried, I was talking to myself. Thankfully, I had
learned a key lesson from my adventure, that the real purpose
of it all is to live "happily ever after". I also learned on my
adventure that you never fail until you give up.

The Castles of Ism

Religion, a balm to man's existence during periods of peace and stability, becomes the bane of man's existence during times of turmoil and change.

A Meeting with the Goddess in all her splendor is a mind-blowing escape from Mythlock. It is a liberation of the mind from existing inadequate myths, and it comes with enormous adaptive advantages. We acquire a broader perspective allowing us to see more clearly. We gain self-knowledge and self-awareness. We can gain an understanding of the emotional pattern inherent in the creative process itself, which is a key to escaping Mythlock in the future. We can become immune to the trap of Mythlock. If we experience ourselves as the authors of the myths of our minds, we can see that it is not the events of life but our responses to those events that count, and we can take control of our lives and banish hopelessness forever. These are just some of the adaptive advantages that can be gained by the hero of an emotionally successful Monomythic Adventure.

Most people select another avenue, a "Rescue from Without". They seek and find a comprehensive solution to their problem within the philosophies and religions of the world. The most prevalent comprehensive adaptive strategies existing in the world are religions. But there is a price that must be paid for the comforts and inspirations of any group-wide adaptive strategy. The cohesion that holds together the members of a group or religion requires agreement on the basic principles upon which the group is founded. A like belief system is the core. Over the years religions clarify and solidify the tenets of their beliefs.

In the early years of most religions, there are always struggles against heresies. This is a common evolution of religion. Slowly over time they solidify, codify, and firmly establish a set of beliefs. This is the hallmark of stability --- commonly held beliefs and habitual or even ritual responses to life's daily challenges. While this clarification of beliefs increases the cohesion of the group it also decreases the flexibility of the adaptive strategy. Religions develop orthodoxy. The result is Mythlock. And as a religion becomes mythlocked so do its hundreds, thousands or even millions of members become mythlocked. This is not a problem if a culture continues in a world without significant change. But change, some say, is the only constant, and in our current era change is the only reality.

Orthodoxy is essential because a religion cannot survive if its members are constantly spouting heresies. To preserve cohesion, common beliefs are essential. Most of us are born into a religion and hardly ever give any thought to the theology behind it. We just accept it and listen attentively on Sundays to the minister's application of theology to matters of everyday existence. In matters of theology, we bow to the wisdom of our leaders. In areas of theology, we let our religious leaders do our thinking for us. This is not a problem until something changes and the orthodox adaptive strategy fails to provide us with effective responses to a changing world.

When confronted with an adaptive challenge that lies beyond the capabilities of our existing knowledge and experience to resolve, we need a Monomythic Journey. But the inward-looking evaluation of existing beliefs is impossible for a large mythlocked group of orthodox thinkers. Because there are hundreds, thousands, or even millions of minds, the inertia renders religions almost incapable of change. The creative genius of the founder of the religion who attempted to devise an effective adaptive response to their age gives way to the strategy of the bureaucrats. Their goal is not an effective adaptive response to new challenges but the preservation of the existing ideas and beliefs of the established orthodoxy.

As environmental influences continue to change the landscape of a culture, and no positive strategy arises from the orthodox perspective, discomfort grows. So religious leaders follow the standard path of all human beings and scan the environment for the source of the problem. The leaders of religion look external to themselves for a source of the problem and always find a scapegoat or two to replace their discomfort with anger. It is at this point that religion also fails to achieve its goal of a wonderful life for its adherents and becomes the bane of man's existence.

My research of the life and times of Jesus revealed that Jesus' mission was not to save the world, which was a tenet added later by Paul, but to liberate the minds of his countrymen from the superstition beliefs of Jewish orthodoxy of his age. First-century Israel was a country in turmoil. The Romans had changed the world. They had established peace, Pax Romana, throughout the Mediterranean creating commercial opportunities never before possible. New, modern, Hellenistic ideas were breaching insular tribal beliefs and being picked up by the young. Israel had just been conquered by Rome and some of the natives were chaffing under the subjugation. They were blind to the new possibilities of the times. The Israeli culture was in turmoil.

> Uprisings in the recent past, brutally crushed by
> the Romans,
> Are still fresh memories.
> Violence begets violence and hatred for the
> Romans flourishes.
> All in Palestine who do not hate Rome are
> branded as collaborators.

Although crushed, rebellion still seethes beneath
the surface.
Tax collectors for Rome, branded as collaborators,
assuage their feelings
by becoming rich.
They line their pockets, and they use the power
of Rome to enforce their greed.

Poor families are driven from the land and made
destitute by the greed of others
Widows are robbed of their incomes, driven
into the streets, and left destitute by the greed
of others.
It is a time when the rich get richer and the poor
get poorer.
It is a dangerous time because desperation breeds
violence.

The rich, and those dependent upon their
patronage, decry the immorality of the age.
They do not see in their greed and selfishness a
source of the desperation of others.'
The land seethes with discontent.
Out of this turmoil factions arise, with their own
prescriptions for the problems of Israel. (Blake
Whitman 149-50) (This quote is taken from my
book, The Greatest Hero, published under the
pseudonym, Blake Whitman.)

There were several factions in first-century Israel each with
its own adaptive strategy to address the nation's problems.
The Pharisees sought to re-establish the purity of religion by
enacting rules and regulations for everything. They believed
that should everyone adhere to god's precepts, as defined by
them, god would spring to the rescue and drive the Romans

from the land and restore Israeli hegemony. The Zealots on the other hand sought to help god drive the Romans from the land through acts of violence but all it did was provoke brutal Roman retaliation. Then there were the Essenes who saw the hand of god in the turmoil of the times bringing about the establishment of his kingdom upon the earth, so they ran off to the mountains to await the end of the world.

It was into this environment that Jesus was born. It was into this environment that he tried to introduce his adaptive strategy, which was to teach the Adaptive Response so people could work out their own adaptive strategy in this new environment and create for themselves a prosperous, wonderful, happy life. The Romans had enforced unprecedented peace on the Mediterranean, a boon to commerce, and new Hellenistic ideas out of Greece provided exciting new possibilities. But the theocratic leaders of Israel, rather than looking inward and devising a new and more appropriate adaptive response, looked external to themselves for the source of the problem and Scapegoats were identified. The Judean hated the Samaritans because the Samaritans did not believe as the Judean believed. Everyone hated the Romans. And anyone who proposed a reasonable adaptive response was immediately branded as a heretic or collaborator.

The religious leaders, unwilling or unable to devise a creative response to the inevitable tide of change, fought it at every step. And those who had abdicated their rights of thinking for themselves became a resource for manipulation. Their minds were turned to hatred and their actions to violence against those who did not believe as they believed. This was the reality that Jesus attacked:

> "Woe to you, teachers of the law and
> Pharisees, you hypocrites!

You shut the door to the *Kingdom of
Heaven in men's faces.
You declare your beliefs as fixed, final and
definitive and with threats of blasphemy,
You block the doors for the timid to the glories
of Heaven.
You yourselves do not enter, nor will you let
others pass.

Woe to you, teachers of the law and
Pharisees, you hypocrites!
You travel over land and sea gathering
converts, and when found,
You make them twice as evil as you.
You collect to yourselves an army of sycophants
and imbue them with hatred
Blake Whitman 378

*In the quoted text the mythic images of the
Kingdom of Heaven and the Garden of the
Goddess are synonymous.

Anyone who sought a creative response to the challenges of
the time was branded a heretic or collaborator. And those
who blindly followed their leaders watched as the way of
life they cherished was destroyed by the changes and they
were filled with anger and hatred towards those scapegoats
identified by their religious leaders. As history shows, Jesus
was unsuccessful in changing the minds of his countrymen,
and the adaptive strategies of the other Jewish factions were
incapable of providing a viable option. Sadly, Israel remained
mythlocked and within eighty years Israel was destroyed and
the population dispersed.

There is a mythic bird called the Phoenix who lives for ages and then burns itself to death, rising fresh and young from its own ashes. This is a mythic image that delineates the fate of cultures that fail to adapt to the inevitable changes that arise over time. The culture self-destructs in the fruitless battle to stem the tide of change and religion provides the mindless motivation that creates the major reactionary bulwarks against change. When religion marshals the minds of its followers in the battle against change, the result is the tragedy of countless lives lost in the conflagration.

The Middle East today looks a lot like first-century Israel. The political structure of most countries is tribal whether headed by warlords, dictators, kings, or religious leaders. Their cultures are in turmoil largely because the tribal infrastructure is inadequate for the needs of the people in the twenty-first century. Also in the Middle East, religion is more integrated into the political and social fabric of the society than in most places and as a result, the pressure of change is seen as an attack on Islam.

The West may have a tolerant attitude toward religion, but the West is the primary source of all the technological and commercial changes that are disrupting these cultures. The West is also the source of radical ideas like women are equal to men and homosexuals have a right to life. This makes the West the perfect Scapegoat. "Islam is under attack by the West". The mindless motivation of religious Scapegoatism against change is even more strikingly displayed as Muslims kill Muslims because of the schism between Sunni and Shia within the Islamic religion. And if the word evil has any meaning, it applies to those religious leaders who convince children to strap explosives around their bodies and walk into crowded marketplaces and blow themselves up. When the trauma of change affects a culture, religion is always ready to provide scapegoats and fan the flames of the conflagration. A bright light in this smoky darkness of the Middle East was the Arab Spring where the younger generation most affected by the changes in modern technology were examining their cultures and demanding change. Whether these cultures eventually evolve successfully, or follow the pattern of the Phoenix, with today's modern communications technology we will get to watch it on TV.

The world is changing because of the proliferation of communications technology and worldwide economic integration. No country or culture is immune. We live in a Global Village. Lest we in the West look smugly at those cultures in the Middle East, we are also in the throes of rapid change. And the cultural beliefs of the West seem equally incapable of creatively developing adequate responses to these discomforting changes. When cultural change disrupts stability, many flee to the comfort of religion or dream of a return to the past where nostalgia makes everything look wonderful.

Organized religion is incapable of undertaking a Monomythic Journey and their habitual response is the identification of scapegoats as the source of the problem. A cultural phenomenon of the 1990s, which identifies the selected scapegoats of religion in the U.S., is the Promise Keepers, an Evangelical Christian international conservative organization for men.

> Openly antigay, antiabortion, and antifeminist, Promise Keepers members rally against the standard targets the Christian right loves to hate: atheism and evolution and the perceived moral degradation of America that comes from them. (Shermer, Location 948)

Lest we believe these actions in the U.S. are benign protests, don't forget the righteous anger fanned in the less stable minds of some adherents that have resulted in the murder of doctors who performed abortions. Anger and intolerance are the hallmark scapegoat-driven responses of religion to cultural change. The United States has become the most religious of the so-called first-world states. Thankfully, currently, at least, the U.S. is not totally dominated by the radical religious right, although they may be the loudest faction. It can only be hoped that one of the world's greatest democracies will find a way to adapt to a changing world without following the evolutionary pattern of the Phoenix.

An escape from Mythlock is a step outside existing myths including the limiting myths of culture and religion. Because of the tendency of religion to want to preserve the cohesion of its beliefs, new ideas, and their proponents are seen as dangerous and become the scapegoats. Our Mythic Heritage notes this danger. Remember Actaeon? Actaeon was the young hunter who encountered the Goddess in all her naked splendor and was transformed into a beautiful and powerful stag. Actaeon experiences a shattering of his cage of Mythlock. He is reborn; he sees his whole world in a new light and is changed, he returns to an unchanged world and is torn to pieces. This is a challenge to the returning hero, returning changed to an unchanged world. The crucifixion of Christ is a real-world historical case of the danger of the return described by the myth of Actaeon. Religion, while a balm during periods of peace and stability, becomes the bane of man's existence during times of change unleashing death and destruction upon the world and particularly upon any who challenge its orthodoxy. Religions tend to become the primary Castles of Ism in a changing world.

The Illusion of Truth

All we believe may not be true but merely beautiful.

A returning hero eager to share his or her boon generally encounters an indifferent world. This indifference can turn to hostility because people are generally not sympathetic to the disruptive influence of creative enthusiasm. Most people opt for the comforts of conformity. Conformity is stability. The world may throw obstacles in the path of the returning hero, but the real Challenges of the Return do not arise from the world. The real and most dangerous challenges always arise from within. It is always the returning hero's response to the Challenges of the Return that spells success or failure of any Monomythic Adventure.

A very dangerous moment of the Monomythic Adventure occurs in the final steps along the revelatory path. The moment of inspiration is an escape from an existing myth of the mind. At the moment of escape, the mind becomes fluid, and a new perspective is devised casting new light on all that we perceive. At this moment the goal of the conscious mind is to expedite the dissipation of the initiating discomfort. So, our conscious mind takes the new information revealed through the new perspective and quickly devises new meaning. The motive of the conscious mind is to come up with an answer for the dissipation of discomfort, not the discovery of truth, or even better a more appropriate adaptive strategy. For the conscious mind, any answer will do as long as it dissipates the discomfort. This is a key fact to remember to avoid the potentially dangerous trap of the Illusion of Truth.

The pre-inspirational crises can be much more than merely uncomfortable. A crisis precipitated by a tragedy can be excruciatingly painful. Thrashing about in Mythlock, the pain can be unrelenting, and the conscious mind can become desperate to find anything at all that will relieve the suffering. Images of death arise, and the conscious mind can seize upon them as the only means of escape from the torment. This can lead to the tragedy of suicide. Similarly, at the moment of an Escape from Mythlock, the mind is fluid, stability is shattered and for some, this is as frightening as shooting rapids in a leaky boat. The conscious mind in desperation seeks an answer and grabs and clings to the first rock it finds arising out of the murk. Any answer will do, any port in a storm, as long as it dissipates the angst.

The beauty of any answers that rescues you from torment or terror can emotionally seize hold of the mind and lock it into an almost inescapable state of Mythlock. With that event comes the absolute certainty that the fixed and final truth has finally been discovered. This is a dangerous state because the mind becomes impervious to rational thought. This is the danger of the Illusion of Truth. It is a danger that can produce humorous or tragic results.

A charismatic leader becomes convinced of the absolute truth of the fact that behind a snowy comet streaking through the evening sky is a hidden spacecraft coming to rescue the faithful from a world he believes is on the brink of destruction. This is humorous. This is insane. No one in their right mind would believe such an off-the-wall idea. But this is a charismatic leader with followers who have abdicated the use of their own minds to the acceptance of the vision of their leader. So, their leader convinces them of the truth of his vision. Depressed by the belief that the end of the world is at hand they look for hope anywhere. They prepare themselves for embarkation.

They don't pack their bags. They kill themselves because their leader, caught in the Illusion of Truth, tells them that death is the boarding pass to this hidden spacecraft. This is tragic. This is also not fiction. This happened in South America in 1978 when the American cult leader, Jim Jones, convinced his followers of his new truth (Jonestown Massacre, November 18, 1978, Britannica).

A charismatic leader caught by the Illusion of Truth with blindly dedicated followers is a prescription for disaster and there are many historical references to this type of disaster. The realm of the mind is a realm of the unfettered imagination and is the source of the most brilliant, ingenious, and astounding discoveries as well as the source of the most idiotic ideas.

> Imagination is at once the source of all hope and
> inspiration but also frustration. To forget this is
> to court despair. (Koestler 213)

The goal of the conscious mind is to dissipate discomfort. Once this task is accomplished there is no incentive to go on, no reason to ascend further up the Stairway to the Stars in search of better understanding.

The psychological reality underlying the story of the Prince of Lonesome Isle, who took us up the Stairway to the Stars, illustrates the flexibility of a fluid mind. The Prince mounted on his shaggy pony shot past the end of the Castle of Tubber Tintye;

> "sprang from its back through an open window,
> and came down inside, safe and sound. The
> whole place, enormous in extent, was filled with
> sleeping giants, and monsters of the sea and
> land." (Campbell 109-110)

This is the magical, mental realm where fear can breed monsters of the mind. Carefully the Prince makes his way to a great stairway. At the head of the stairway, he goes into a chamber where he finds the most beautiful woman he has ever seen asleep on a couch. Psychologically, he takes the new perspective discovered on this landing of the Stairway to the Stars and devises new meaning and it is beautiful.

For some reason, the Prince remains curious, and he proceeds up the stairway to another chamber and a more comprehensive perspective. Again, he devises a new meaning, and it is even more beautiful than that which has come before. As we know the Prince proceeds up the Stairway passing twelve chambers containing ever more beautiful women until he discovers the Queen of Tubber Tintye herself. The psychological equivalent of an actual ascent up the stairway is extremely exciting. The mind is fluid during the experience of inspiration. We find an answer to a question that is bothering us and it's beautiful. If for any reason we do not accept this answer, immediately our conscious mind devises another. If we don't accept this one, immediately another answer appears. It happens so fast. The mind just flips through answers, like through a Rolodex, one after the other producing wild trains of thought. But the trip to the top of the Stairway to the Stars is not the most frequent path followed by a Monomythic Adventurer.

Most adventurers stop at the first chamber enthralled by the beauty of the first answer devised. There is no reason to go beyond that because the goal of the conscious mind has been achieved. Discomfort is dispelled. Most often the conscious mind's first interpretation is accepted as the truth. Most often this answer is enough for us to determine an appropriate Adaptive Response. Most often the returning hero is unaware that another answer, perhaps a better answer, even exists. This ignorance coupled with the beauty of the answer in hand exposes the returning hero to the danger of the Illusion of Truth.

The Illusion of Truth is a challenge that arises from the very nature of the human perceptual organs. The gift of the Goddess is always merely a new perspective. Using this perspective and the new information revealed, the conscious mind devises new meaning. This is an emotionally cathartic event. The discomfort of not knowing is replaced by the joy of understanding. The intensity of the emotions is proportional to the discomfort that prompted the quest. The sense of beauty arising from the new meaning devised becomes the measure of the value of that understanding in meeting immediate adaptive needs. The more beauty, the stronger the sense of certainty that at last the final, definitive, and absolute truth is known. This certainty can be burnt into the mind of the hero by the intensity of the emotions of the moment.

It is easy to forget the realities of human perception, particularly, when riding a wave of inspiration. All the meaning we perceive is a product of the myths of our minds. A new perspective reveals new information opening up new possibilities. Our conscious mind, eager to restore stability and dissipate discomfort, takes this new information and devises a new understanding, a new myth of the mind. This myth creates order to the chaos of inspiration. Change the myth and we change the meaning perceived. This is the reality of human perception.

> If Perceptive Organs vary, Objects of Perception
> seem to vary:
> If Perceptive Organs close, their Objects seem to
> close also. (Blake 471)

If we change the myth of our mind that we use to order the raw data of our senses and it changes the meaning we perceive; where does truth reside? If the beauty of an idea is a measure of the validity of a perception towards meeting immediate adaptive needs and a different and more beautiful answer is always possible up the Stairway to the Stars, where does truth reside? The perception of absolute truth, it turns out, is beyond the capabilities of the human perceptual organs. The human perceptual organs are incapable of the perception of any truth independent of the myths of our minds. Truth is an illusion.

The Monomythic Adventure is a journey into the realm of the mind. This is a realm of all possibilities and the gift of the Goddess is always merely a new way of looking at things. With this new perspective, our conscious mind devises a new myth of the mind. These myths can birth the most insightful, brilliant, and profound ideas or just as easily, the stupidest ideas imaginable. There are no guarantees.

In science, if the myth or theory proposed matches close enough with reality, we have success. Newton and Einstein were lucky.

> Because their theories related both to their own internal worlds and also the external world, we rate them as men of creative genius. If there had been no such link with reality, their hypotheses would have been indistinguishable from psychotic delusions. (Storr 178)

There are no guarantees. The meaning we perceive is produced by the myths of our minds and these myths are the rationalized creations of our conscious minds.

A mind in the throes of inspiration is a fluid mind with an unfettered imagination. In this state anything is possible. It is always possible for a returning hero to be convinced of the absolute truth of an absolutely stupid idea.

> False inspirations and freak theories are as abundant in the history of science as bad works of art; yet they command in the victim's mind the same forceful conviction, the same euphoria, catharsis, and experience of beauty as those happy finds which are post factum proven right. (Koestler 330)

While emotionally we may feel certain that a final, definitive, and absolute truth has been discovered, the reality is that many more chambers filled with many more beautiful, more comprehensive visions await further up the Stairway to the Stars. Our conscious mind cares nothing about the validity of an idea. The goal of the conscious mind is the dissipation of discomfort. And, if the answer is beautiful enough it will meet our adaptive requirements. Truth plays no part in this equation. Truth is an Illusion.

I have heard it said that the majority of our ideas and attitudes to life are fixed by the age of eight. This means that most of the myths in our minds, which determine the meaning that we perceive, are the creations of an eight-year-old. No wonder we occasionally behave like children. This reality should be humbling. It should teach us to beware of certainty and becoming caught by the Illusion of the Truth.

It is easy to recognize those who are caught in the Illusion of Truth. It is evident in their strident certainty. Their ideas are not offered as new perspectives to broaden our minds and open us to new possibilities but as fixed, final, and definitive truths. Their goal is not the liberation of the mind but the locking of minds into their cage of Mythlock. Their stridency also tends to be loud and intolerant. These are the false prophets of religious mythology. Strident certainty is a simple litmus test to detect those caught by the Illusion of Truth.

All knowledge is tentative. The evolution of understanding that transpires within a single mind can be seen in the evolution of ideas in human history. A man stands outside watching the morning sun peak its head above the eastern horizon. Slowly it rises to its zenith and later, slowly and surely, it sinks below the horizon in the west. The pattern is simple; he has observed it many times. But nightly some fear the dark and worry that the sun may not rise tomorrow. They do not understand the reasons behind the pattern and find it difficult to live with uncertainty. Within the imaginative realm of his mind and inhabiting a world believed to be populated by gods, this man devises an understanding. The divine Phoebus daily mounts his fiery chariot and makes his regular trek through the heavens. There is even a role for man to play. Praise god and we will be saved. Mankind's devotion ensures that Phoebus will never fail us. The simple reality-based contents of the sun's daily trek is now understood. A myth of the mind creates meaning for the sun's daily motion. Anxiety is dispelled now that the truth is known.

Years pass and the pantheon of gods is banished. Now a new god, an omniscient, omnipotent god rules the universe. This is the "real" god that created the earth and all its wonders as a home for his chosen creature, mankind. The earth, the home of his chosen, stands at the center of the universe. The sun, the moon, and a vast canopy of stars revolve around this earth-centered universe, moved and maintained forever by the hand of god. There is no anxiety; god will protect his chosen. A new myth creates an understanding of the simple pattern of the daily rotation of the sun. Anxiety is banished because now the truth is known.

More years pass and this truth has become an unconscious invisible myth in the minds of the human population. Another man gazes at the sky. With an accumulation of careful observations, anomalies are discovered in the existing belief -- anomalies that cannot be explained by the dominant paradigm. These anomalies cause discomfort in our curious scientist. He undertakes a Monomythic Adventure and within the Garden of the Goddess, he discovers a new myth, which again creates a new understanding of the simple pattern of the rotation of the sun. The real truth is finally known. Of course, Galileo was forced to recant his discovery that the earth was not the center of the universe in the face of religious opposition. Recanting seems a reasonable adaptive response when the alternative is death. But the genie is out of the bottle and soon everyone comes to know this new truth. There is no anxiety, except in the minds of religious bureaucrats who see a refutation of their monopoly on truth as a diminution of their authority. God still controls the movement of the planets, so all is well, even if man is no longer at the center of the universe.

Still, more years pass and a harmless apple, as the story goes, falls on Newton's head. He has a revelation, a new myth is devised, Newton's idea of universal gravity. A large metaphoric string of gravity extends from the sun to the earth and like a ball tied on the end of a string spins around your head, the earth spins around the sun. The motion of the earth keeps it from falling in and the string of gravity keeps the world from spinning off into space. Here is an understanding based on science that explains everything. Finally, the definitive, final, and absolute truth is known. No reason for anxiety, universal gravity will maintain the motions of the planets. If you find this less than reassuring, you can always maintain your belief in the myth that god's hand still holds the strings of universal gravity. Either way with this understanding, anxiety is kept at bay.

Then one day another man, gazing at the sky through the window of his patent clerk's office discovers some new anomalies as yet unexplained by Newton. Using the tool of mathematics he gains a new perspective. A new myth is born. Newton was wrong. The sun does not hold the Earth in orbit by a string of gravity. Instead, the sun creates an enormous gravity well, a large curvature in space, and the earth rotates around this hole -- its motion keeping it from falling in and the curvature of space keeping it from spinning off into space. Finally, the absolute, definitive truth is known and if you believe this you are a victim of the Illusion of Truth. Count on it, in the future some latter-day Einstein is going to discover yet another new final and definitive truth. All knowledge is tentative. All we ever know is merely our conscious mind's best guess going with the information at hand. Always there is yet another chamber waiting to be opened up the Stairway to the Stars.

Understanding varies depending upon perspective. Even Twentieth Century science has discovered that a new way of looking at things produces different but often equally valid results. Take a ray of light. Look at it one way and it appears to look and behave like a wave rippling through space. This perspective explains many interesting phenomena, but not all. Look at light as a particle, a proton, speeding through space and this perspective explains many other interesting phenomena. Both can't be true in any final, definitive, and absolute fashion. Both are merely different ways of looking at things, different myths that produce different yet equally valid results.

> There is no absolute knowledge. And those who claim it, whether they are scientists or dogmatists, open the door to tragedy. All information is imperfect. We have to treat it with humility.

That is the human condition, and that is what quantum physics says. (Bronowski, 353.)

Meaning arises from perspective and one perspective does not invalidate the meaning arising from another. A key revelation of these tales from our Mythic Heritage is that all that we know and believe is a rationalized creation or fantasy of our conscious mind deemed adequate by the feelings of the heart. It is a humbling realization that our conscious mind, which we consider the end-all and be-all of who we are, is merely a tool in the service of our emotions. But it is also empowering to know that if the rationalized fantasy that we believe is not achieving its objective, the creation of a successful, happy life, all we need do is book ourselves in for another Monomythic Adventure.

The Magic Flight

It is not the world that determines the success or failure of a returning hero, but the hero's response to the Challenges of the Return.

Over and over again I have described the emotional pattern of the Monomythic Adventure as being precipitated by a problem or crisis and the feelings of discomfort. This was the nature of my experience. But our mythic heritage documents adventures precipitated by feelings other than depression or despair. Narcissus, for example, suffered from the 'Is that all there is syndrome.' Rather than a particular crisis requiring an answer, he sought something more in his life. Similarly, Phaethon's adventure was not precipitated by a crisis but by an eagerness to prove his paternity. Proof of paternity in a tribal culture could very well be a driving force in the life of a fatherless boy. In both these mythic tales, the Adventure was not so much thrust upon the hero as sought. Rather than feelings of discomfort, desire is the primary emotional instigator of the adventure, whether the desire for something more like Narcissus or the desire to find an answer to a long-sought question like Phaeton. Desire can also be a harbinger of a Monomythic Adventure. Our Mythic Heritage reveals that we need not sit around awaiting a crisis but can be proactive in seeking the Adventure to expand our horizons or enrich our lives. Since feelings and emotions drive the Monomythic Journey, this completely alters the nature of these Adventures.

Within the Garden of the Goddess, our feelings and beliefs mold the landscape and determine the nature of the imagistic world. Based upon our feelings, the Goddess can be a Hag or a Seductrice. Where the Adventure is not thrust upon the hero by a crisis but willingly sought, prompted by desire, the entire nature of the Adventure is transformed. This gives rise to another genre of mythic tales where the Garden no longer becomes the place where the favor of the Goddess is sought but instead, it becomes a realm where the boons and treasures are hoarded and hidden by ogres and jealous gods. The treasure must be retrieved through skill, stealth, and daring. This is the genre of the Magic Flight, which reveals some new Challenges of the Return.

The flight from a pursuing ogre or god is a common element of the genre. The Russian story of Morgon-Kara is an example, and it illustrates an important challenge of the return.

> The Buriat of Irkutsk (Siberia), for example, declare that Morgon-Kara, their first shaman, was so competent that he could bring back souls from the dead. And so the Lord of the Dead complained to the High God of Heaven, and God decided to pose the shaman a test. He got possession of the soul of a certain man and slipped it into a bottle, covering the opening with the ball of his thumb. The man grew ill, and his relatives sent for Morgon-Kara. The shaman looked everywhere for the missing soul. He searched the forest, the waters, the mountain gorges, the land of the dead, and at last mounted, "sitting on his drum," to the world above, where again he was forced to search for a long time. Presently he observed that the High God of Heaven was keeping a bottle covered with the ball of his thumb, and, studying the circumstance, perceived that inside the bottle was the very soul he had come to find. The wily shaman changed himself into a wasp. He flew

at God and gave him such a hot sting on the forehead that the thumb jerked from the opening and the captive got away. Then the next thing the God knew, there was this shaman, Morgon-Kara, sitting on his drum again, and going down to earth with the recovered soul. The flight in this case, however, was not entirely successful. Becoming angry, God, immediately diminished the power of the shaman forever by splitting his drum in two. And so that is why shaman drums, which originally (according to this story of the Buriat) were fitted with two heads of skin, from that day to this have had only one. (Campbell 199-200)

Morgon-Kara was successful, but a price was paid. The life of our hero was changed forever. How a hero responds to the challenge of this change, spells success or failure of his or her Adventure.

The creator of the Morgan-Kara folktale has a message for future Monomythic Adventurers. You will be changed by the adventure. A successful return requires dealing successfully with these changes. The shaman's power was diminished, symbolically his drum was altered forever. As a psychological parallel, imagine, for example, an unpretentious scientist working quietly for years in some back room who makes a great scientific discovery. Suddenly she is thrust into the limelight. She has discovered a hidden "truth" of science and now the world is beating a path to her door. Her life is changed. She loses some of the power she may have had over her own life. If shy, she may find the attention discomforting. She has achieved success; she has discovered a new scientific 'truth' but a price is extracted; her life is changed. How she deals with this change is the measure of her success or failure. If she wishes to achieve the real goal, of living life "happily ever after," it is clear that she needs to adapt to her altered world. She has a need for yet another Monomythic Adventure.

The most famous mythical story of the Magic Flight genre is the story of Prometheus. Prometheus stole fire from the gods and bestowed this powerful boon upon mankind. God was extremely upset by Prometheus' trickery, so he had him chained to a rock and regularly an eagle arrived to eat his immortal liver, which constantly replenished itself. Prometheus was condemned to eternal torment. In the mythological language of religion, this is called 'the retribution of the gods'. It is used as a threat by the Threshold Guardians of religion to keep the timid from venturing beyond the boundaries of the tribe.

What message is the creator of this myth trying to communicate to future Monomythic Adventurers? Imagine being a young physicist in the early half of the twentieth century who discovers $e=mc2$.. Within this equation is an inexhaustible supply of power to heat, light and run the industries of the world. You envisage a utopian future full of abundance and wealth. Of course, politicians and military men with their focused perspectives, take this wonderful idea, create a nuclear bomb, and devastate Hiroshima and Nagasaki. You are horrified with this use of your discovery and become tormented by the devastation that you believe you have unleashed upon the world. You suffer the torment of regret. This is a warning that the creator of this myth is passing on to future Monomythic Adventurers. Einstein did not succumb to this Challenge of the Return and went on to live a full life in spite of what the world made of his discovery. It is not the world that determines the success or failure of a Monomythic Adventure but the hero's response to the Challenges of the Return and tormenting oneself with regret is hardly a successful adaptation.

Another less than successful response to the Challenge of the Return and documented in Our Mythic Heritage, is one that can actually arise during the return of any Adventure, not just the Magic Flight variety. Continuing with our example of the discoverer of e=mc2, imagine that as the young scientist you recognized the potential of your discovery to wreak havoc upon the world. You decide that the world is not ready for your discovery. You decide to keep it hidden. You become a hoarding ogre. To make sure that word will not slip out about your dangerous secret, you retire to the woods and become a hermit. There are many reasons why one might become a hermit, but from most perspectives, hermithood is hardly a successful adaptation. To achieve anything like a 'happily ever after' ending, another Monomythic Adventure is definitely required. This new Monomythic Adventure may reveal to you that people probably won't even understand what it is you have discovered. Or you may learn that hoarding knowledge is fruitless because if the idea has any validity, it will eventually come out anyway. Or the Adventure may teach you, that although predicting the future is easy, it hardly ever turns out as you imagine.

There is another response that can trouble the return of those who experience their adventure as a Magic Flight. The treasure was stolen from the ogre and the ogre is in pursuit to retrieve his treasure. A treasure stolen once can be stolen twice. The hero begins to fear that this new treasure will be taken from him. But remember, in the emotional realm 'fear breeds monsters of the mind'. This monster is paranoia. Paranoia is an absolutely wonderful example of the power of a perceptual filter to create meaning and hide contrary evidence. While the hero worries about someone stealing his idea and the distrust of paranoia becomes a monster of the mind, the reality usually is that the hero will be lucky if he can find anyone who will even listen to his idea. The world is generally skeptical, indifferent, or even hostile to new ideas. Paranoia is also definitely not a successful adaptive strategy.

The Monomythic Adventure is symbolic of the Adaptive Response. It is a creative response to a challenge of adaptation. Its purpose is survival or success, and true success is achieved when we create an adaptive strategy that leads to a happy, joyful life. A crisis may initiate the Adventure, but this is not the ideal path. Ideally the hero, knowing that an answer lies within, consciously, and willingly embarks upon a journey to retrieve the treasure. The Challenges of the Return can themselves give rise to many a new adaptive challenge requiring yet another Monomythic Adventure. This is an obvious reality since there is no such thing as a single adaptation that makes life perfect forever. The world is constantly changing, and we change, and we have to adapt to these changes. Successful living requires many Monomythic Adventures. This is the secret, as we shall see, of the real genius heroes, the Masters of Two Worlds.

There is one more tale of the Magic Flight genre that I want to include because it illustrates the wild and wonderful creativity of a fluid human mind, and it also identifies the gift of the Goddess directly with inspiration.

> The Welsh tell, for instance, of a hero, Gwion Bach, who found himself in the Land Under the Waves. Specifically, he was at the bottom of Lake Bala, in Merionethshire, in the north of Wales. And there lived at the bottom of this lake an ancient giant, Tegid the Bald, together with his wife, Caridwen. The latter, in one of her aspects, was the patroness of grain and fertile crops, and in another, a goddess of poetry and letters. She was the owner of an immense kettle and desired to prepare therein a brew of science and

inspiration. With the aid of necromantic books she contrived a black concoction which she then set over a fire to brew for a year, at the end of which period three blessed drops should be obtained of the grace of inspiration.

And she put our hero, Gwion Bach, to stir the cauldron, and a blind man named Morda to keep the fire kindled beneath it, "and she charged them that they should not suffer it to cease boiling for the space of a year and a day. And she herself, according to the books of the astronomers, and in planetary hours, gathered every day of all charm-bearing herbs. And one day, towards the end of the year, as Caridwen was culling plants and making incantations, it chanced that three drops of the charmed liquor flew out of the cauldron and fell upon the finger of Gwion Bach. And by reason of their great heat he put his finger in his mouth, and the instant he put those marvel-working drops into his mouth he foresaw everything that was to come, and perceived that his chief care must be to guard against the wiles of Caridwen, for vast was her skill. And in very great fear he fled towards his own land. And the cauldron burst in two, because all the liquor within it except the three charm-bearing drops was poisonous, so that the horses of Gwyddno Garanhir were poisoned by the water of the stream into which the liquor of the cauldron ran, and the confluence of that stream was called the Poison of the Horses of Gwyddno from that time forth.

"Thereupon came in Caridwen and saw all the toil of the whole year lost. And she seized a billet of wood and struck the blind Morda on the head until one of his eyes fell out upon his cheek. And he said, 'Wrongfully has thou disfigured me, for I am innocent. Thy loss was not because of me.' 'Thou speakest truth.' said Caridwen, 'it was Gwion Bach who robbed me.'

"And she went forth after him, running. And he saw her, and changed himself into a hare and fled. But she changed herself into a greyhound and turned him. And he ran towards a river, and became a fish. And she in the form of an otter-bitch chased him under the water, until he was fain to turn himself into a bird of the air. She, as a hawk, followed him and gave him no rest in the sky. And just as she was about to stoop upon him, and he was in fear of death, he espied a heap of winnowed wheat on the floor of a barn, and he dropped among the wheat, and turned himself into one of the grains. Then she transformed herself into a high-crested black hen, and went to the wheat and scratched it with her feet, and found him out and swallowed him. And, as the story says, she bore him nine months, and when she was delivered of him, she could not find it in her heart to kill him, by reason of his beauty. So she wrapped him in a leathern bag, cast him into the sea to the mercy of God ...." (Campbell 197-8)

This story of the Magic Flight is a marvelous illustration of the ingenious creativity of the human mind, whether exhibited in the world of everyday or within dreams and myth. Gwion Bach taps into the vast resources of his mind and imagination and escapes again and again. Of course, Gwion Bach is eventually caught and eaten but within the realm of dreams and myth, this is not disaster. This is merely the death that precedes rebirth. An adventurer returning from an Adventure devastated by an encounter with the images of death does not understand the nature of the symbolic realm.

> The creative mind knows how to draw on archetypal symbols without degrading them by misplaced concreteness. (Koestler 357)

Escape from Mythlock

The rebellious nature of young people often arises from an emotional yearning for a Monomythic Adventure.

The human animal is not built for a world in a constant state of change. In the early years of life, young children devise strategies that allow them to adapt, flourish and survive in the world into which they were born. In time, this learning, having proven successful, becomes habitual and slides below the threshold of conscious awareness, and becomes the invisible myths we live by.

Of course, the world does change over time and discomfort arises for the generation that adapted to the world that has now passed. Then, a new generation comes along, builds their adjusted adaptive strategies, and all is well for them, and the older generation dies off. This human cultural adaptive strategy only works when change is very slow. But cultural change hasn't been that slow since before the industrial revolution.

In our world, cultures undergo multiple major changes in the lifetime of a single individual. As long as the world confirms our unconscious knowledge, we feel comfortable and at home. If the world changes or our unconscious understanding is challenged by change, we feel uncomfortable and threatened. In our current world, uncomfortable, is the feeling that dominates. This discomfort prompts our emotions to tell the computer in our heads to find out what's going on. The brain races off and analyzes the situation in light of all our knowledge and experience. But the knowledge and experience available were built for a world that disappeared 20 years ago. So, for most of us, there is no escape from the disruption of change and discomfort persists.

Who we are and how we feel determines the nature of a Monomythic experience. Our feelings draw the landscape, and our motivation molds the events of the Adventure. But a Monomythic Adventure is always a trip into the mind with the ultimate goal of returning with a new perspective. The Magic Flight variety of the Monomythic Journey is prompted by desire, the desire for something more. While desire is still the instigating emotion, the motivation is less towards a goal than it is an escape from an uncomfortable situation.

An example of this type of folktale is Grimm fairy tale number seventy-nine.

> "A little brother and sister were playing by a spring, and as they did so suddenly tumbled in. There was a waterhag down there, and this waterhag said, 'Now I have you! Now you shall work your heads off for me!' And she carried them away with her. She gave to the little girl a tangle of filthy flax to spin and made her fetch water in a bottomless tub: the boy had to chop a tree with a blunt ax; and all they ever had to eat were stone-hard lumps of dough. So at last the children became so impatient that they waited until one Sunday, when the hag had gone to church, and escaped. When church let out, the hag discovered that her birds had flown, and so made after them with mighty bounds.
>
> "But the children espied her from afar, and the little girl threw back her hairbrush, which

immediately turned into a big brush-mountain with thousands and thousands of bristles over which the hag found it very difficult to climb; nevertheless, she finally appeared. As soon as the children saw her, the boy threw back a comb, which immediately turned into a big comb-mountain with a thousand times a thousand spikes; but the hag knew how to catch hold of these, and at last she made her way through. Then the little girl threw back a mirror, and this turned into a mirror-mountain, which was so smooth that the hag was unable to get over. Though she: 'I shall hurry back home and get my ax and chop the mirror-mountain in two.' But by the time she got back and demolished the glass, the children were long since far away, and the waterhag had to trudge back again to her spring. "(Campbell 201)

The children fall into a well. They enter the Garden of the Goddess, but it doesn't look like a Garden at all. Rather than a plain old Hag, the Goddess is a Waterhag and the Garden reflects her realm. Remember when we enter the Garden, we are not yet free from the impact of the meaning created by the myths of our minds. We are initially still mythlocked. The children enter the realm of the waterhag and everything is an emotional reflection of the real world they inhabit. The children are trapped in a boring, meaningless, existence. Endless, useless labor is their fate, hauling water in a bottomless bucket, cutting trees with a dull ax, and their only reward, "stone-hard lumps of dough". There is no scope in this environment for enthusiasm or even childish play. Life is going through the motions without emotion.

The children inhabit a real world reflected in the mythic images of the Waterhag's realm. There is no scope for creativity or fun. Conformity is the rule. This is a picture of an extremely restrictive home or cultural environment. This is an environment geared to turn children into automatons living their lives like puppets on the strings of the myths of their parents. But in this Grimm fairy tale, the children become impatient. Intuitively, they know that life has more to offer. Believing there must be something better, the children seek escape. The children rebel.

A man, a workaholic, strives for success. His trophy wife is a dedicated assistant in her husband's endeavors. He achieves a position of power and all the accouterments of wealth, yet happiness escapes him. His accomplishments lose their value. He becomes discontent with his trophy wife. Unaware that the solution lies within and is accessible through a Monomythic Adventure, unhappiness persists. Although the man and his wife present a shallow façade of happiness to the external world, unhappiness permeates the home. Place a child in this environment. Now children may listen to the words of their parents, but they learn through observation. Despite all the parents have accomplished, all the child sees is unhappiness and the child wants out. Like the children in the fairy tale, the child rebels.

How does this mythic tale, this inner mental/emotional Adventure of the children help their real-life Escape from Mythlock? In their minds, the decision is made to flee. Their flight is facilitated by every creative means at their disposal. They use a brush; a comb and finally a mirror, every strategy they can devise until they discover one that lets them escape. This new perspective gained, or the lesson learned in this Adventure is that escape is possible through creative action. Once this inner realization is achieved the children are equipped to return to their real-life restrictive environment to face the challenges of an Escape from Mythlock.

The rebellion of spirited children in an overly restrictive environment is an almost conditioned response. If a child does not rebel, they become conformist automatons confined by the limited boundaries of the myths of their parents. They look cute, tiny little adults so mature for their age sucking up the compliments of adoring adults. These children become what they believe others want them to be. They learn to live their lives, like their parents, according to the dictates of others. This ill equips them to function effectively within the changing world of their peers. All children grow up in a world different from their parents. Change is the constant. When an earlier adaptive strategy, which has ceased to function effectively, is forced upon the young either they become dependent, or they rebel. The young need to break free from earlier ideas to create new strategies to deal with the new challenges of their times.

In the above tale, the children wait until the hag has gone to church before making their escape. This is a purposeful association by the creator of the folktale because religion is a primary source of the conformist myths that define any culture. During periods of cultural upheaval, there can be a growth in religious participation as people seek the comfort of the familiar and this growth strengthens the ranks of the reactionary forces attempting to stem the tide of change. Religion is a bulwark against change. Religion becomes the refuge of those desperate to preserve the myths of the past because blinded by these myths they see the alternative as chaos. They fight to preserve the past because they cannot see any alternative except disaster and god is on their side. As Threshold Guardians, religion uses fear to limit the explorations of the young to the safe and sanctioned boundaries of the tribe. This Grimm folktale deals with two children breaking free from their restrictive environment. But when a whole culture exhibits a restrictive nature, the pattern of response delineated by the acts of these two children can become the pattern of behavior for a whole generation.

In the nineteen sixties, we witnessed, on a cultural scale, the psychological event symbolized in this Grimm fairy tale. The nineteen fifties were a conformist decade. All the new labor-saving appliances could be ours as long as we worked hard and kept our noses clean. This was an age that gave birth to McCarthyism, where even thinking about possible alternatives to the capitalist system was blasphemy. Free speech became a victim of conformity. This was also the age of television's perfect families. Weekly, these television programs presented the ideal life until a whole generation believed that the perfect house behind a perfectly white picket fence was the perfect ideal. A normal family with normal problems was viewed as dysfunctional. The unconscious, habitual, invisible myths upon which society was founded were accepted assumptions and never mentioned or questioned in these TV shows. These TV shows dealt with major human crises like surviving a case of the zits or the life-crushing disappointment of not getting the lead in the school play. These families became the promoted icons of the perfect life -- a house with a white picket fence where "father knows best".

Children of the fifties were inculcated with these images of perfection; regardless of how unrealistic they were. Natural, disruptive enthusiasm was curbed by cultural conformity. But the children became impatient, wondering whether there was not a more joyful approach to life. They began to question things. The black civil rights movement in the southern United States hit the television screens exposing the dark underbelly of this perfect world. What the children had been told and believed was exposed as a lie. Trust was shattered.

In the sixties, the lid blew off. A generation rebelled. A whole generation experienced the emotional pattern of an Escape from Mythlock as delineated by Grimm fairy tale number seventy-nine. There are many whose eyes still light up with excitement contemplating the Adventure that was the sixties.

The rebellion of a whole generation of young people is not unique in history. In Christian mythology, there is a brief mention of a parallel situation. The first century, as we have already noted, was a time of radical cultural transformation. New Hellenistic ideas were permeating the theocratic culture of Israel, which was grating under the control of a foreign power. While the local religion mounted a campaign to stem the tide of change with restrictive rules and customs, a rebellious younger generation created a sixties-like rebellion.

> To what can I compare this generation? They
> are like children sitting in the marketplaces and
> calling out to others:
>
> We played the flute for you,
> and you did not dance;
> we sang a dirge,
> And you did not mourn. (Matthew 11:16-17)

Although written two thousand years ago this is a picture of the hippies of the sixties singing in the streets. This was also the time and place of the activities of the West's greatest hero. Jesus was accused of being a glutton and drunkard by the religious authorities of the day. If long hair was the in thing, he might have been called a 'long haired hippie'. One thing is clear. His sympathies were clearly with the rebellious youth.

> You must not think that I have come to bring
> peace to the earth; I have not come to bring peace,

but a sword. I have come to set a man against his father, a daughter against her mother, a son's wife against her mother-in-law; and a man will find his enemies under his own roof. (Matthew 10:34-36)

Jesus' goal was to break his countrymen free from Mythlock so they could devise new and exciting responses made possible by the "Pax Romana."

Notice that it tends to be the young against the old, a boy against his father, and a daughter against her mother because the young are always less securely trapped in the myths of the age. The young, while rebelling against the fixed beliefs of the past, are busy creating their own fixed beliefs, which in their turn will be rejected by some future generation. This is a repetitive cycle. Where this rebellion of the young runs into extreme reactionary opposition, violence can flare. We saw a manifestation of this in Tenamin Square in China and it has happened in Iran where the young are rebelling against the stifling restrictions of the ruling theocracy. In fact, in the spring of 2011, it happened all over the Middle East where the young rebelled against either the stifling restrictions of theocracy or the stifling oppression of the tribal structure of their countries whether headed by warlords, dictators, kings, or religious leaders. They knew there was something better and they wanted it.

Mythlock is the habitual state of the adult human. Mythlock is a description of a stable culture. Change may be intellectually acknowledged as reality but very few people emotionally revel in the turbulence of constant change. Radical change of any kind is hardly tolerated in most cultures. For most of us:

> The future is regarded not in terms of an
> unremitting series of deaths and births, but as
> though one's present system of ideals, virtues,
> goals and advantages were to be fixed and made
> secure. (Campbell 60)

The result is that cultural evolution follows the path of the Phoenix. The old culture is violently destroyed so the new culture can evolve. The violence in our current world is a reflection of this path of cultural evolution.

Now, imagine a world where everyone is aware of this seemingly endless, repetitive, and destructive cycle of Mythlock, rebellion, followed by reactionary violence. It is a future where everyone understands the process. Even those motivated by greed and sustained by power will understand their time is passing and their best bet is to aid the transition or get out of the way. In this future, new ideas are accepted for what they are, merely possible answers to the challenges of the times. This is a world where good ideas, in time, are accepted because they meet a need. Bad ideas, in time, wither away because they fail to meet society's needs or cause more troubles than they resolve. This is a culture without the strident certainty of those demagogues who believe they know what's right for everyone. In this glorious utopia, human culture evolves without the need to litter the streets with bodies to bias the evolution of an idea. This is paradise. But this fantasy will never come about until each of us understands the nature of our own creativity and the realization that cultural change is the only constant.

Masters of Two Worlds

Genius is not some inherited trait bestowed upon some and denied others, but merely a habit of mind and emotion.

It's easy to see the tentative nature of knowledge when exploring the history of ideas but it's not so easy to see the tentative nature of all our own cherished ideas and beliefs. It is not so easy to absorb and see the implications of the idea that the myths of our minds create the meaning we perceive. It's hard to grasp all the implications of the words; we behold what we've become. And unless we have personal experience of the reality of inspiration, where new light is suddenly cast upon all we see, it is even harder to understand that if we change the ideas and beliefs within our minds, we change the meaning we perceive. The creativity of the human mind is without limits. There is no reality for which it cannot devise an understanding. But the perception of fixed, final, and definitive truth is beyond the capabilities of the human perceptual organs.

The external world is not the source of any of the meaning we perceive. All the meaning we perceive is a product of the myths in our minds. Change the myth and we change meaning. All we know and believe is merely our conscious mind's best guess going with the information at hand. All knowledge, including that which resides within our own personal repertoire of knowledge and experience, is tentative. We need the myths of our minds to create meaning for the raw data of our senses and if we use a different myth we perceive a different meaning. Truth is an illusion. No matter how many times or ways you say it, the reality is hard to grasp. It is the source of some strange and cryptic pronouncements.

> To know is not to know; not to know is to know
> (Campbell 236).

Think about it for a minute. The implications of all this are that the myths of our minds are fiction. They are rationalized constructs of the conscious mind created to help us understand reality. Their goal is to facilitate successful adaptation. Regardless of the meaning that they create if we are surviving and living a reasonably happy life, they are achieving their objective.

There is a breed of heroes, called the Masters of Two Worlds, who live the reality of these esoteric pronouncements. One of them, Aristotle, an acknowledged genius of the Greeks, is quoted as saying, 'I know that I know nothing.' Here is one of the world's greatest heroes acknowledging the tentative nature of the myths of his mind. These Masters of Two Worlds are the geniuses of the world, and the essence of their genius is intimate familiarity with the Monomythic Journey. They know and live the creative process. They live a creative life. They have intimate familiarity with the world within. These geniuses know that within the Garden of the Goddess lies all the human heart could ever desire. And they don't need a crisis or even an overwhelming desire to cross the threshold into the Garden. For them the crossing is habitual.

> Freedom to pass back and forth across the world
> division, from the perspective of the apparitions
> of time to that of the causal deep and back --
> not contaminating the principles of the one with
> those of the other, yet permitting the mind to

know the one by virtue of the other -- is the talent
of the master. (Campbell 229)

To the Masters of Two Worlds, the creative process is habitual,
and they clearly understand the symbolic nature of the inner
realm and how to use it to understand the outer world.

The Masters of Two Worlds understand the imagistic, metaphoric
nature of the realm of their minds and do not adulterate these
images with literal interpretations. They understand that the
images of understanding and the images of communication
are symbolic.

> Symbols are only vehicles of communication;
> they must not be mistaken for the final term,
> the tenor, of their reference. No matter how
> attractive or impressive they may seem, they
> remain but convenient means, accommodated
> to the understanding. Hence the personality
> or personalities of [the Goddess] -- whether
> represented in trinitarian, dualistic or
> unitarian terms, in polytheistic, monotheistic,
> or henotheistic terms, pictorially or verbally, as
> documented fact or as apocalyptic vision -- no
> one should attempt to read or interpret as the
> final thing. ... Mistaking a vehicle for its tenor
> may lead to spilling not only of valueless ink, but
> valuable blood. (Campbell 236)

The Masters of Two Worlds laugh sadly at the Mythlocked
individuals who interpret the myths of their minds as fixed,
final, and literal truths.

These geniuses know that the gift of the Goddess is always
merely a new way of looking at things. They know that the

myths they devise create meaning to the raw data of their senses. And no matter how beautiful the resulting vision may be, they can always create another myth to produce a different meaning potentially just as beautiful. They revel in the pleasures of new perspectives.

> The Cosmic Dancer, declares Nietzsche, does not rest heavily in a single spot, but gaily, lightly, turns and leaps from one position to another. It is possible to speak from only one point at a time, but that does not invalidate the insights of the rest. (Campbell 229)

Genius knows that different perspectives can lead to the devising of different meaning by the conscious mind. Through the myth of one lens, light is a wave, and it explains many phenomena. Through myth of another lens, light is a particle, and this explains many phenomena. Meaning arising out of one perspective, as beautiful as it may be, does not invalidate the meaning arising out of another. The Cosmic Dancers lightly leap from perspective to perspective to get a better, more comprehensive understanding of reality, but never declare that the truth has been found.

Genius also revels in the pleasures of creativity. This is the pleasure of inspiration. This is the pleasure of the creative act. This is the pleasure of learning. It is exciting to suddenly learn something new in a situation where you thought you knew it all. It is exciting to see new possibilities that before you never knew existed. This is the dance of genius and also a reason genius is frequently attacked for inconsistency. How can one be consistent when gazing through one perceptual filter and seeing faces, while gazing through another reveals a vase? It is said that consistency is the bane of small minds, but it is the result of the fallacious belief that there is only one, single, final, and right way of looking at anything. This is the result of the Illusion of Truth.

All our understanding is a symbolic representation of reality. Its value lies in how effective it is in facilitating adaptation. Truth has no role. If the myths we believe in work, allow us to function and live wonderful happy lives, they are achieving their goal. Many people have strongly held beliefs that others may see as ideas that are destroying the current culture of their nation. As long as these beliefs facilitate successful adaptation for the individual or the group, their myths are achieving their objectives. The real stupidity arises not from the ideas but from the juvenile conflict based upon the belief that 'my myth is better than your myth'. Real stupidity arises when two fictions taken as absolute truths fight for supremacy with the blood of their believers and totally fail to achieve their objectives of creating a wonderful happy life for anyone. Hence our streets are filled with protestors pushing to change the chaos of our current culture while the other side is fighting to hold back the tide of change.

The idea that all our cherished beliefs are fiction is frightening for many. Most of us require, for our peace of mind, certainty, and certainty is available for those caught by the Illusion of Truth. Most of us are caught in the trap of Mythlock and blinded by the Illusion of Truth and living wonderful happy lives. If all the adaptive challenges we face are adequately handled by the existing myths in our minds, we can live wonderful lives. Even genius not blinded by the Illusion of Truth adopts defined adaptive strategies. They merely acknowledge that all they believe may not be true but merely beautiful. They also know that when an adaptive strategy starts to fail and chaos persist, it is time for a new adaptive strategy to arise.

If everything we know is fiction, how can we ever decide what to believe? We have to believe something! We have to make choices, or we become paralyzed by indecision. Genius is not paralyzed by indecision. Genius willingly absorbs and adopts new myths to explore their utility. But should a better idea arise, genius has no compunction casting the old coat aside and dawning a new garment. New wine needs new bottles. Genius is not afraid of ambiguity because genius knows how to determine the value of any idea.

Within Our Mythic Heritage and out of the mouths of the genius heroes of the past comes a method to determine the value of any idea. We have already discussed this but it bears repeating. You can tell the worth of an idea by the fruit it bears.

> You will recognize them by the fruits they bear. Can grapes be picked from briars, or figs from thistles? In the same way, a good tree always yields good fruit, and a poor tree bad fruit. A good tree cannot bear bad fruit, or a poor tree good fruit. And when a tree does not yield good fruit it is cut down and burnt. That is why I say you will recognize them by their fruits. (Matthew 7:15-20)

When an idea or belief ceases to function effectively, failing to achieve its goal of successful, happy, adaptation, the geniuses of the world know to cut it down and burn it or cast it aside like an old coat.

The world that human beings inhabit is a creation of the externalization of the ideas and beliefs residing within the minds of men and women. The culture we inhabit is ruled by the accepted ideas and beliefs of its members. These beliefs shape the world through ritual and the definition of acceptable actions, interactions, and reactions. If a culture creates a paradise for its members, the myths guiding that culture are doing their job. If a culture is not creating a paradise for all of its members, then there are myths within it that need to be set aside. The quality of life and the happiness of its members are the fruits of the ideas and beliefs upon which it is founded. You can tell the value of these ideas not by the meaning they create but by the fruits they bear.

How does genius explore the fruits of new ideas? They know that an intellectual understanding of an idea is not enough. Not until an idea is absorbed, embraced like Naill embraced the ugly hag, or put on like a pair of sunglasses, do the implications of an idea become visible. To evaluate an idea the Masters of Two Worlds become heartfelt adherents exploring all the positive implications of their adopted idea. They feel as real adherents feel to know as a real adherent knows. With their fluid minds and positive emotions, they see the positive implications that draw adherents.

> It is the mark of an educated mind to be able
> to entertain a thought without accepting it.
> (Aristotle)

To explore the underside of an idea the Masters of Two Worlds adopt the negative feelings of the opponents of a belief. Using the fluidity of their minds, the genius explores an idea from as many angles as possible to thoroughly determine the potential fruits that it may bear. Genius enters the Garden and uses the creative process to determine the possible fruits of an idea. These geniuses are everywhere if you look for them. In our crazy world, Susan Liautaud in her book, *The Power of Ethics: How to Make Good Choices in a Complicated World*, outlines how to separate the good fruit from the bad fruit.

There are many areas in life where we are guided by ideas and beliefs that are impossible to objectively verify. We take these ideas on faith. These are some of our most cherished beliefs. Take for example the idea of reincarnation and karma. Reincarnation is the belief that after death we return to life in new bodies repeatedly until through some act of salvation we are liberated from this repetitive cycle. Karma, the sum of a person's actions in this or previous lives, is the determining factor for the quality of the life into which we are reborn. If we are good, we are rewarded in our next reincarnation. If we are bad, we are punished in the next. What are the fruits of the ideas of reincarnation and karma?

Proponents say that a belief in reincarnation and karma promotes goodness. It motivates us to be good. Be good to others including the animals of the world in this life and you will be rewarded in the next. And, if you are really good in this life you can escape the repetitive cycle of rebirth and enjoy the rewards of eternity. This belief also provides an understanding of reality. Look around your world. There are the rich and the poor, the comfortable and the desperate, and those that are happy and those that are sad. The belief in reincarnation and karma provides perfectly logical explanations for the inequitable distribution of wealth and happiness in the world. The wealthy were good in their past life and the poor are being punished for past transgressions. This belief creates understanding and justification for all the inequities in the world.

It creates justification for a class society. This idea justifies the belief that the class into which you are born and not any innate human value determines your value as an individual human being. The idea provides cultural justification for doing nothing while children live in abject poverty. This is the fruit of any belief that values life after death more than life itself. The struggle and suffering of the poor are their just rewards for past misbehaviors. It is the will of god. The extremes of poverty and wealth in some cultures where the belief in reincarnation and karma are held is in part a reflection of a culture created by the externalization of this belief. The perception of truth is beyond the capabilities of the human perceptual organs, but the value of an idea can be determined not from the meaning it creates but from the fruit it bears. This leads to another piece of wisdom known by the Masters of Two Worlds. To change the world, you need to change the ideas and beliefs within the minds of men and women.

There is an experience of writers that illustrates the positive fruits of an idea almost independent of the myth used to create an understanding of it. It is a specific event that occasionally occurs within the inspirational experiences of writers. We have all heard of 'writer's block' but this is at the opposite end of the scale. While writing and struggling to clarify an idea and find the right words to express it, a writer may experience an event that is a lot like someone whispering into their ears exactly what they want to say in words that say it perfectly. This moment of inspiration is an extremely pleasurable phenomenon that can lead to a torrent of creativity.

There is a myriad of consciously devised explanations for this phenomenon. There is one belief that has been around before recorded history. This is the idea that occasionally the wisdom of our dead ancestors is passed on to the receptive mind. There are modern groups who practice what they call "channeling". Muhammad, the founder of Islam, is purported to have had an entire book, the Koran, dictated to him by angels. Jesus, apparently, had frequent conversations with his dead father. In Canada, we had a very successful prime minister who nightly discussed world affairs with his dead mother. Her advice must have been good because he had a long and successful political career. Some believe as Carl Jung believed that these inspirational ideas leak through to receptive minds from the 'collective unconscious'. Some believe that it is merely a fluid mind birthing beautiful ideas through the act of creativity. One thing is clear. No writer who has ever experienced anything like this will deny its reality regardless of the myth they use to explain it. All we believe may not be true but merely beautiful.

The realm of the human mind is an emotionally fluid, imagistic realm. It is not a world of ridged, fixed, final, and definitive truths. It is not meant to be a cage of Mythlock. The world of our minds is the home of the myths, the ideas, and the beliefs we use to guide our lives. This is the source of those perspectives that we use to order the raw data of our senses creating the meaning that we perceive. Different perspectives expose different facts and reveal different options allowing us to devise different responses to the ever-changing challenges we face. A fluid mind is blessed with limitless possibilities because it is the source of answers to challenges, we have yet to imagine. Human survival is dependent upon this ability. Human survival is dependent upon the Adaptive Response. Within our mind lies all the human heart could ever desire. Constantly tapping this inner resource is the secret of the Masters of Two Worlds.

The genius of children is obvious. They learn so much in such a short time. We can see the openness in their wide-eyed wonder. We can see the joy of learning in their smiles. Of course, in their formative years' proper nutrition and a loving family life is essential as is adequate sensory stimuli. A sense of security must also be maintained to prevent fear from inhibiting a child's natural curiosity. With these environmental essentials in place, a child's natural genius will flourish.

Children experience life through their feelings, which is why they are so emotionally vulnerable. They feel things and then create understanding with their conscious minds. They test the adequacy of their understanding and modify it as necessary until it seems correct. With every successful application of a learned concept, its reliability is confirmed until it becomes habitual and is added to their repertoire of knowledge and experience. Children eventually grow up to become teenagers who know it all. Teenagers become adults caught in the trap of Mythlock. Their knowledge, a boon to survival, becomes a barrier to creativity because the conscious mind sees no need to seek understanding when it believes it already knows it all. How can the genius of a child survive the transition to adulthood? How does the genius of a child survive the transition to adulthood so that the child becomes a Master of Two Worlds?

Children learn through feelings. We all learn through feelings. To live an experience is to experience it emotionally. It is the emotional pattern of events that gets burnt into the mind and memory. Touch fire with your hand and pain results. We learn not to stick our fingers into the fire. But we can learn this without having to burn ourselves. We can learn vicariously. We learn by experiencing a situation in the reality of human emotional response whether we experience it in reality, in dreams, or while sitting on the lap of our mothers listening to heroic tales. Children approach life through their feelings; they empathize with the situation or the characters of the story and experience the adventure in the reality of human emotional response. They experience it as real.

I remember my nephew in a movie theatre watching the movie, The Dark Crystal. The climax was reached, and all the hero had to do was throw a shard of glass to shatter an evil spell. Time was running out and the director strung out the tension of the moment until it was just too much for my nephew. He jumped up in the dark and quiet theatre and yelled out, "Throw the damn thing!" A child exposed to fairy tales who experiences the emotions of the moment that takes the hero through the trials of an adventure to a successful conclusion is introduced to the emotional pattern inherent in the creative process. Exposure again and again through a variety of fairy tales and folklore to the pattern of creativity will make the child familiar with the Monomyth. An understanding of the Monomythic pattern, an intimate emotional familiarity with the creative process, is a primary characteristic of the Masters of Two Worlds.

Athletes practice. Great athletes practice a lot. They may make adjustments to their technique to optimize results but then they practice and practice to make it perfect. They practice until the right technique is second nature and occurs without conscious thought. They practice until what they need to do becomes habitual. The adaptive response is a technique of mind and emotion. Here too, practice makes perfect. The more the child is exposed to the pattern inherent in the creative process the more familiar the child becomes with the pattern. When the child recognizes this pattern within their personal experience, the child learns to look within themselves for answers. The more they look within themselves for answers and the more success they achieve with this strategy, the more practice the mind gets. With enough practice and enough success, it becomes habitual. When the creative process is habitual and occurs without conscious thought, we have genius.

> One is not born a genius, one becomes a genius"
> (Simone de Beauvoir)

Genius is not some inherited trait bestowed upon some and denied others, but merely a habit of mind and emotion.

The Monomyth is a pattern that delineates every hero's earthly or unearthly quest. It is a common story with infinite variety.

> The mythological hero, setting forth from his common day hut or castle, is lured, carried away, or else voluntarily proceeds, to the threshold of adventure. There he encounters a shadow presence that guards the passage. The hero may defeat or conciliate this power and go alive into the kingdom of the dark (brother-battle, dragon-battle; offering, charm), or be slain by the opponent and descend in death (dismemberment, crucifixion). Beyond the threshold, then, the hero journeys through a world of unfamiliar yet strangely intimate forces, some of which severely threaten him (tests), some of which give magical aid (helpers). When he arrives at the nadir of the mythological round, he undergoes a supreme ordeal and gains his reward. The triumph may be represented as the hero's sexual union with the goddess-mother of the world (sacred marriage), his recognition by the father-creator (father atonement), his own divination (apotheosis), or again -- if the powers have remained unfriendly to him -- his theft of the boon he came to gain (bride-theft, fire-theft); intrinsically it is an expansion of consciousness and therewith of being (illumination, transfiguration, freedom). The final work is that of the return. If the powers have blessed the hero, he now sets forth under their protection (emissary); if not, he flees and is pursued (transformation, flight, obstacle flight). At the return threshold the transcendental powers must remain behind; the hero re-emerges from the kingdom of dread (return, resurrection).

> The boon that he brings restores the world (elixir).
> (Campbell 245-6)

Some myths follow the Monomyth from beginning to successful conclusion. Others may dwell upon single aspects providing warnings of dangers that lay along the path (Narcissus, Actaeon).

> Many tales isolate and greatly enlarge upon one or two of the typical elements of the full cycle (test motif, flight motif, abduction of the bride), others string a number of independent cycles into a single series (as in the Odyssey). Differing characters or episodes can become fused, or a single element can reduplicate itself and reappear under many changes. (Campbell 245-6)

The variety is as infinite as the minds, experiences, and cultural backgrounds of the creators of myth. In this lies the richness of Our Mythic Heritage.

The psychological reality, imagistically presented in the stories of heroes, is the 'adaptive response'. The 'adaptive response' is a pattern that delineates the creative process whenever existing knowledge and experience prove inadequate to a challenge at hand. It is the pattern inherent in simple problem-solving, flashes of inspiration, or mind-blowing revelatory events. It is the essence of the religious experience. Feelings of discomfort begin a churning of the mind. The emotions vary from the mild discomfort of a nasty problem to the desolate emptiness of the loss of all meaning and purpose. The emotions provide the power to break out of locked perceptual habits (Mythlock) and prod the conscious mind to seek relief (a Monomythic Journey). Or the desire for more or to make things better can motivate the hero. If fear (Threshold Guardians) does not bar the way, if the emotions are not vented through anger upon some innocent external entity (Scapegoatism), or an answer is not discovered in the external world (Rescue from Without), the inner journey proceeds. Armed with confidence (Magic Amulets), attention is directed inward, and the solution is sought within one's own mind (The Garden of the Goddess). A simple inspiration (Boon) leading to a simple answer to a simple problem may be the reward or much, much more. Buffeted by the emotions of crisis, the inward search can lead to one's life flashing before one's eyes (Looking Glass). One may be forced to confront the unleashed emotions of guilt, regret, or anger (Judgment Day), and in the process, the emotions are groomed for the Adventure ahead. Or the forgiveness found in front of the Looking Glass may be the boon itself, a liberation of the mind from debilitating guilt or anger. The mind becomes fluid, and it becomes possible for a Meeting with the Goddess or even an ascent up the Stairway to the Stars (Nirvana). The contents of the experience vary as widely as the mind, experience, and cultural backgrounds of the adventurer. This is the source of the richness of Our Mythic Heritage.

The Masters of Two Worlds know that if any problem arises, major or minor, to look first within their own minds for an answer. They know, whenever a problem arises in their lives, the solution lies in yet another Monomythic Journey.

> Seek first the Goddess and all else will follow
> For within the Garden of the Goddess lies all the
> human heart could ever desire.

The goal of the Monomythic Journey is happiness. Where does happiness lie in a world, like ours? Rapid change is shattering any hope of stability and the human specie is the source of all this change. New, creative inventions are changing all aspects of our world. Wild creativity is producing new products that perform amazing tasks. Our world is in constant change and the human animal is the source of all this endless change.

But the most devastating events in our current world are not the results of human creativity. Most arise from our inability to successfully adapt to all these changes. The human animal is not built for a world in a state of constant change. In the early years of life, young children devise strategies that allow them to adapt, flourish and survive in the world into which they were born. In time, this learning, having proven successful, becomes habitual and slides below the threshold of conscious awareness, and becomes an invisible myth we live by. We become Mythlocked and blinded to new options and new possibilities. If we examine the current state of our world, in light of all that has been discussed in the previous chapters, we can see how our failure to adapt to change is playing out in the turmoil consuming our world.

Let us first examine one man-made existential threat to our specie, and our natural, repetitive response. The facts below were taken from a Scientific American excerpt from Spencer R. Weart's article, *The Discovery of Global Warming* (Harvard University Press, 2008). In 1896, the Swedish scientist, Svante Arrhenius, published an observation that the increased burning of fossil fuels was adding carbon dioxide gas to the Earth's atmosphere and creating a "greenhouse effect" that would raise the temperature of the world and could have far-reaching implications. Svante's warning was laughed off or welcomed by those who saw a few degrees of Global Warming as a good thing. Perhaps Svante didn't elaborate enough with a clear picture of the potential implications, because the implications were seen as irrelevant, and in the case of Svante's warning, the Goddess was perceived as a Hag. In the 1930s, it was discovered that the United States and the North Atlantic regions had warmed significantly during the previous half-century. In

1988, the hottest summer ever recorded (Most since have been even hotter.), the prediction was made that by the year 2000, unprecedented global warming would become apparent.

The response was immediate and vehement. The Goddess was declared a Hag. Corporations and individuals who opposed all government regulation began to spend millions of dollars on lobbying, advertising, and publishing "reports" that mimicked scientific publications, in an effort to convince people that there was no problem at all. But droughts leading to endless wild forest fires and rivers of rain leading to devasting floods, have become annual events around the world. When the reality of a perspective is constantly placed before our eyes, it becomes hard to neglect. Hopefully, the devastation of Global Warming can be mitigated by the actions of the people of this world before it is too late.

But Global Warming is not the most dominant disruptive event in our current world. Our cultural world is changing and the horrific implications of our failure to adapt are visible everywhere. The saddest of all is what happens to those people who try and fail to find an understanding to relieve their angst. They find no solution to relieve their discomfort, and their brain suggests the only way is to end it all.

> Globally, close to 800,000 people die from suicide every year. That's one person every 40 seconds. Due to the stigma associated with suicide – and the fact that it is illegal in some countries – the figure is also likely to be an underestimate, with some suicides being classified as unintentional injuries. (ourworldindata.org)

My eyes tear contemplating this terrible loss. Clearly, such toxic "solutions" are glaring failures of adaptation.

A good portion of the disruption and turmoil in our world stems from the battle between the ideas of the past and those of the future. Misogyny, a paternalistic attitude, that has existed in every human culture in the world is now being exposed. Women traumatized by the abuse they received are using the new communication technologies to discuss their trauma. The 'Me-too' movement has given voice to the oppressed. Their success is noteworthy in that even the courts are now recognizing the abuse rather than sluffing it off as they have in the past as 'boys just being boys'. The oppressors are going to jail, and other potential oppressors are seeing that the world has changed, and their habits must change also. More importantly, the young are recognizing the horror of this attitude and misogyny is not becoming an invisible myth of young minds.

The proliferation of new electronic communication capabilities is giving voice to others who have suffered over the centuries from horrific inculcated cultural norms. We now celebrate "Pride Day", where differences are celebrated rather than being hidden away. In some cases, we still have far to go. Sixty-seven countries in the world still criminalize homosexuality and half a dozen maintain the death penalty as punishment (Human Rights Watch). In Canada, the history of the government's treatment of the indigenous population has finally made the news. Children torn from their families were confined in residential schools, the last of which closed in 1996. Their cultural heritage was erased from their minds, and many were abused by the priests. Hundreds of unmarked graves are still being found in the fields surrounding these schools. Modern communications technologies are exposing the horrors of the past, and in some cases revealing their source, the invisible myths of our minds.

Our young are now adapting to the new Global Village we inhabit. Where in the past we only saw young, slim, white, beautiful, Anglo-Saxon males and females in commercials, we now can see a more realistic reflection of the Global Village. This is the new world that our young are adapting to. Xenophobia, homophobia, misogyny, and racism are being exposed and denigrated for what they are, faulty myths of our minds and no longer tolerated.

Happiness may be hard to find in such turbulent times. But I am reminded of the words of my university history teacher when we were studying the Greek Golden Age. He said we would not have wanted to live in that age because there were wars going on and turmoil boiled everywhere as new and often wonderful ideas, like democracy, fought the old and dying ideas of the past. Democracy was an answer devised in that era to prevent the terrible chaos of a changing world on human culture. The Greek world was in turmoil as old ideas past their prime battled against new ideas to deal with the new problems. The battles were disruptive and violent, much like they are today. Democracy, an idea from the geniuses of that era, was to put ruling power in the hands of the majority, so as new ideas arising to solve the problems of the present were absorbed by the young, a point would be reached when the new ideas were accepted by the majority without the need for a violent and destructive revolution. Perhaps if our current political leaders got rid of the 'first past the post' voting system so that power in our parliaments reflected the majority, we might get rid of the partisan bickering that currently dominates politics.

Imagine a world where xenophobia, homophobia, misogyny, and racism were no longer among the invisible myths of the minds of the majority. Women would be able to walk alone at night without fear, rather than parading annually in large groups, carrying flags declaring "Take Back the Night".

247

Imagine a world where young people were taught that 'within the Garden of the Goddess lies all the human heart could ever desire'. Suicide could be greatly diminished. Now imagine that young people were taught that scapegoatism was a destructive misuse of their 'fight and flight response'. So much violence would be banished from our world. Imagine the Phoenix, destroying herself and arising new from the ashes, as a myth from the past and no longer a valid description of current cultural evolution. This would be paradise. Perhaps this world could lie at the end of the current cultural tunnel of torment. Perhaps, in a hundred years or so, people will look back at our age as the Golden Age of the World.

This thought makes me happy.

Bibliography

Baltzly, Dirk, "Stoicism", *The Stanford Encyclopedia of Philosophy (Fall 2008 Edition)*, Edward N. Zalta (ed.), URL = <http://plato.stanford.edu/archives/fall2008/entries/stoicism/>.

Blake, William, The portable Blake. Selected and arranged with an introduction by Alfred Kazin. New York, Viking Press, 1946.

Bronowski, Jacob, The ascent of man. Boston, Little, Brown. c1973.

Brooks, Terry. The sword of Shannara. Illustrated by The Brothers Hildebrandt. New York, Ballantine Books, 1977.

Campbell, Joseph. The hero with a thousand faces. Bollingen Series XVII, Second Edition. Princeton, New Jersey, Princeton University Press, 1968.

Espinosa, Aurelo M. "Notes on the origin and history of the tar-baby story" in Journal of American Folklore, Vol. 43, 1930.

Jung, C.G. Aion: researches into the phenomenology of the self. Bollingen Series XX, Princeton, New Jersey, Princeton University Press, c1959, 1968.

Keats, John. "Ode on a Grecian Urn" in The Norton anthology of English literature, Revised, Volume 2. New York, W.W. Norton & Company, 1968.

Kellogg, Steven. Jack and the beanstalk. Retold and illustrated by Steven Kellogg. New York, A Mulberry Book, 1997.

Koestler, Arthur. The act of creation. Arkana, London, Penquin Books, 1964.

Konstan, David, "Epicurus", *The Stanford Encyclopedia of Philosophy (Spring 2009 Edition)*, Edward N. Zalta (ed.), URL = <http://plato.stanford.edu/archives/spr2009/entries/epicurus/>.

Kuhn, Thomas. The structure of scientific revolutions. Second Edition, Enlarged. Chicago, University of Chicago Press, 1970.

LeShun, Lawrence. How to meditate: A guide to self discovery. New York, Bantam Books. 1975.

Liautaud, Susan with Sweetingham, Lisa. The power of ethics: How to make good choices in a complicated world. New York, 2021.

McLuhan, Marshall. Understanding media: the extensions of man. Signet Books, New York, The New American Library, 1964.

New English Bible: with Apocrypha. Cambridge, Cambridge University Press, 1972.

Ovid. The metamorphoses. Translated and introduction by Mary M. Innes. London, Penquin Books, 1933.

Shermer, Michael. How we believe: science, skepticism, and the search for god. Second Edition, Owl Books, New York, 2003

Storr, Anthony. The dynamics of creation. London, Secker & Warburg, 1972.

Universal dictionary of the English language. Edited by Henry Cecil Wyld. Fourteenth impression. London, Routledge & Kegan Paul Limited, 1961.

Vernon, M.D. The psychology of perception. London, University of London Press, 1962.

Whitman, Blake. The greatest hero: the genius behind the myth. Bloomington, Indiana, Authorhouse, 2007.

Whitman, Edward C. The symbolic quest: basic concepts in analytic psychology. New Jersey, Princeton University Press, Princeton, 1968

Whitman. Walt. The portable Walt Whitman. Selected and with notes by Mark Van Doren. New York, Viking Press, c1945, 1966.

Printed in the United States
by Baker & Taylor Publisher Services